BOILERMAKER MUSIC MAKERS

*To: Lois Gotwals,
With best wishes,
Al Stewart.*

Dr. Albert Pearson Stewart.

BOILERMAKER MUSIC MAKERS

Al Stewart and the Purdue Musical Organizations

by
Joseph L. Bennett

Purdue University
West Lafayette, Indiana

Copyright © 1986 by Purdue Research Foundation, West Lafayette, Indiana 47907. All rights reserved. Unless permission is granted, this material shall not be copied, reproduced, or coded for reproduction by any electrical, mechanical, or chemical processes, or combination thereof, now known or later developed.

Published 1986

Library of Congress Catalog Card Number 86-61175
International Standard Book Number 0-931682-21-5
Printed in the United States of America

For Charlotte Friend Stewart
1910–1984

*No Fun without Music
and No Music without Fun*

Contents

Foreword   xi

Preface   xiii

Acknowledgments   xix

Chapter 1   Carnegie Hall: Breaking into the Big Time   1

Chapter 2   The Preacher's Son   11

Chapter 3   Interlude at Purdue   21

Chapter 4   Down and Out at DePauw   33

Chapter 5   Turning Point   41

Chapter 6   The Music Penthouse   55

Chapter 7   Holiday Magic   65

Chapter 8   Million-Dollar Playhouse   79

Chapter 9	Changes on the Home Front	89
Chapter 10	Victory Varieties	99
Chapter 11	Sirens in White Satin	111
Chapter 12	The Golden Age of P.M.O.	119
Chapter 13	End of an Era	141
Chapter 14	Luhman and Allen: On with the Show!	147
Afterword	159	
P.M.O. Photo Gallery	161	
Appendix A	P.M.O. Hall of Fame Members	173
Appendix B	A Hall of Music Who's Who	174
Index	179	

Foreword

This is a book composed and written by Joseph L. Bennett, the Director of University Relations at Purdue University. The book was sponsored by the P.M.O. Club, an organization of alumni and friends, for the promotion of and benefit to the Purdue Musical Organizations.

My hope and sincere desire is that it will be interpreted by all readers as a history of the beginning of P.M.O. and not as a personal biography.

I am particularly appreciative of the fact that this book has been dedicated to my late wife, Charlotte. She was a source of constant support and encouragement for more than fifty-one years of marriage and shares equally in any success recorded here.

The past few years of close association with Mr. Bennett and Nancy Hansen have been most rewarding to me—for I now know them both, as good personal friends.

I thank them and the P.M.O. Club for putting these statistical facts into print.

Albert P. Stewart

Preface

A lot of people who know more than I do about both Al and music will disagree with me, but I do not consider Al Stewart a musical genius.

I say that, knowing that he turned the Purdue Musical Organizations into the finest and best-known collegiate singing aggregate in America. I realize that he started with virtually nothing—no money, no facilities, no support, and no effective conventional way to develop talent—and brought about the transformation in barely a decade.

I also realize that musicians, entertainers, statesmen and thousands of his own student singers have praised his work both in and out of his presence. A Purdue graduate who had sung with the Glee Club for four years once seized my arm in a grip that told me he had waited a long time to tell this to someone and said: "It's been twenty years, and I still think of Al Stewart every day. I'm not even sure if I like him, but I probably owe him everything I have."

Anyone who inspires that intensity of feeling in others is worth a close look, and that is one of the purposes of this book. The other is to trace the history of the Purdue Musical Organizations. There was music at Purdue before Al Stewart, and it has continued to develop under his successors, Bill Luhman and Bill Allen, since Al retired in 1974. But there is no question that Al is the colossus. It is possible that another individual will yet take Purdue University in a new musical direction that will overshadow everything Al did, but I would be very surprised.

This is not just a question of talent. I began by saying that I didn't consider Al a musical genius, and, though I never asked him the question, I think he would agree with me. He has described himself as just a fair singer and an inadequate piano player. His formal training in music was limited to lessons as a child, a year as a music major at DePauw University, and a short period of study at the American Conservatory of Music in Chicago.

How then could Al Stewart take over a musical program that was obscure, even at Purdue, and in just a few years make it both technically excellent and nationally known? How could he then capitalize on that fame to make Purdue a favorite stopping place for the best-known entertainers of the forties, fifties and sixties? How could he attain enough prominence to serve as master of ceremonies for the Republican Party's national convention? How could he be invited to bring his Glee Club for a private serenade of Franklin Roosevelt at the White House? Why do his former singers still speak of him with awe—usually with love?

The answer, I think is in the convergence of commitment, ability and opportunity. Al Stewart was the right man in the right place at the right time. Trends in popular music were favorable for the development of collegiate singing groups; Purdue's student body was somehow "right" for Al's style of leadership; the university's administration in the person of President Edward C. Elliott gave exactly the right kind of support; and even the absence of a music school at Purdue worked in Al's favor.

None of this is meant to argue that Al Stewart simply blundered into a fortunate situation and reaped the benefits. On the contrary. Had anyone else taken over the University Choir as he did in the early 1930s, music probably would have remained an insular activity at Purdue, perhaps forever. Al Stewart was the catalyst. More than anything else, he was helped by his ability to make a decision and then act upon it. He wasn't always right, but he wasn't afraid of the consequences of being wrong, and that is a far more valuable quality in men than we like to acknowledge.

One of the first things Al told me when we began to talk was that people who thought he had built the Purdue Musical Organizations according to some grand design were dead wrong. He insisted that he had always been an impulsive, rather than a calculating, administrator. "I didn't know what the hell was going to happen next most of the time," he said. "I just tried things, and sometimes they worked."

That boldness of spirit may have been what made Edward Elliott grow so fond of Al Stewart. Their relationship grew into an almost father-son give and take, and Elliott's respect for Al was founded on the music director's refusal to be intimidated by the president. Although at their first meeting, Elliott swore he would never spend Purdue money on music, he ended up spending millions. When he died, P.M.O. was the only university entity mentioned in his will for a cash bequest. He left $1,000. Elliott was an excruciatingly correct man. He set stern limits for conduct at Purdue and he observed them himself. Four years after he retired as president he visited Al on the eve of the Glee Club's first trip to Europe. He handed the director a personal check for $100. "You can't buy a drink with Purdue money," he explained. "I made that rule myself, but you have a right to have a drink while you're over there."

The reputation of the Purdue Musical Organizations was built and maintained with the Varsity Glee Club. Early in his career at Purdue, Al realized that the sound of a young male vocal group was a salable commodity. Although his personal preference was for religious music sung by mixed choirs, he began building the Glee Club to be the headliner for the concerts he was booking on and around campus in the 1930s and early 1940s. A mixture of traditional, popular and sacred music worked well then, and Al would have musical trends in his favor well into the 1960s. He wasn't a Johnny-one-note, though. When World War II thinned the male ranks and restricted travel of men, he developed the Purduettes, a sassy female group, as his headliner and never missed a beat.

Throughout those early days, Al had the growing support of President Elliott, who went from perceiving music as superfluous to Purdue's function to recognizing the enormous public relations benefits of having a student group appear on stages all over the country. Elliott even came to enjoy the Glee Club performances himself.

The Glee Club's early development climaxed with its triumphal performance in a national sing-off produced by Fred Waring in Carnegie Hall. The show gave Purdue national recognition in a way that surprised even its most loyal alumni. How could this prairie college with no school of music produce such great singing? The answer was Al Stewart.

Al knew quite a bit about music, but he knew even more about human nature. Perhaps because of the hardships of his early life, he figured out what a lot of athletic coaches and military leaders always have known: That people—especially young, healthy people—are capable of feats of dexterity and discipline far beyond what they themselves suspect; all they need is a leader who believes in them. Al believed, and he made them believe.

That was why he could put the Glee Club on stage night after night without their knowing for sure what they would sing. It was why he could decide on the spot who would sing a solo. It was why he could produce professional results with amateur singers. He was utterly convincing to his performers.

He also could read an audience as easily as you or I would read a billboard on a highway. I don't know how Al developed that ablity. He couldn't explain it to me, but sometime between peeking out at the hall from backstage and the first intermission, he would know whether "Thanks Be to God" would work better than "Old Man River," and once he had the audience's number, the people were his to enthrall.

Purdue loyalists take an almost perverse pride in the absence of a music school. "Look what we've accomplished without one," we say, and we point to the achievements of P.M.O. and the University Bands. But perhaps a music school would have inhibited the kind of success Purdue has had. Bill Allen told me that one of the things he loves about his singers at Purdue is that they don't know enough to be intimidated by difficult music. If Al had tried to develop his kind of music program on a campus with a music school, he might have found a hostile or—worse—an indifferent environment. His long-time motto, No Fun without Music and No Music without Fun, certainly would not have been welcome at a university where music was taken seriously in an academic sense. Perhaps in that situation he would not have had the privilege of trial and error, and perhaps his peculiar genius would not have flourished.

Did I say genius? I did, and I meant it. I'll hold to my original argument: Al's genius was not music. He loved it, and he chose it as a congenial way to make his living. In so doing, he made it the vehicle for his genius to express itself, but the genius was for leadership. A man named Joe Hendrickson, for many years the sports editor of the *Pasadena Star-News*, wrote in his column once that Al Stewart was one of the greatest all-time coaches. I like the sports association, because long before I read Hendrickson's words, it had occurred to me that had Al exhibited a talent for baseball as a boy, he might have grown up in that sport's milieu and ultimately have managed his beloved Cubs to more pennants than they have achieved without him. He could inspire; he could recognize talent in a young person; and he could bring that talent roaring to the surface. Those gifts would have manifested themselves in sports, in industry, in war. We at Purdue are fortunate that they were applied to music.

As do all great leaders, Al used his people to carry out his mission, but he in turn was used by them willingly. They gave him their talent, their time, their devotion, their obedience. He gave them educations, inspiration, opportunity. The relationships were often stormy, sometimes painful, but the students who followed Al's regimen got back more than they gave, and somehow in the exchange, a kind of love was born, and that's what made the music great.

Acknowledgments

I am indebted to Al Stewart for creating the story of the Purdue Musical Organizations and for sharing it with me. He and Charlotte opened their home and their hearts so that I could hear their story.

Much of the early research for the history was done by Nancy Hansen. She generously shared her efforts, and I borrowed freely from them.

Christine Quimby and Martha O'Farrell provided valuable assistance in locating and selecting pictures. Willis Parker generously shared his personal mementos, and many other members of the Purdue Musical Organizations wrote with information or gave their time in interviews. Jim Emerson of the Elliott Hall of Music provided important research help on the building.

Frank Burrin's biography of Edward C. Elliott was a major source of information and insight on the Elliott administration.

Last, but not least, I am grateful to Donald Carter for creating this book's elegant design and to Janice Becker for her patient and meticulous editing.

Chapter 1

This was how the Purdue Glee Club looked when it arrived by train in New York City in May 1942 for Fred Waring's national singing competition.

CARNEGIE HALL: BREAKING INTO THE BIG TIME

Carnegie Hall was a disappointment. That may have been the first clue that the big time was not too big for them. Forty-three young singers from Purdue University and their tall, commanding director were in New York City to perform in the legendary music hall. That alone was a triumph. They had been plucked from the heartland after Fred Waring, the king of American choral music, had announced a nationwide contest to select the best men's collegiate chorus in the country. Purdue's Varsity Glee Club was one of eight survivors of a national competition that had included hundreds of college groups. Choral music was very marketable entertainment in 1942, and Waring proved it every Monday night on "Pleasure Time," his popular nationally broadcast radio show.

Purdue's young men would face the other seven glee clubs in a two-day sing-off Saturday and Sunday, but at their first rehearsal Friday afternoon, they found Carnegie Hall—Carnegie Hall, the name that was synonymous with great music—a letdown. Their own Hall of Music, dedicated just two years before right on the Purdue campus, was larger by 3,500 seats, and the acoustics were better. Maybe their cow college back in Indiana was better than anybody realized, and maybe they were, too.

The Glee Club had left the depot at South and Second streets in Lafayette Thursday, May 28, 1942, embarking in two private Pullman cars provided by Waring. The director of Fred Waring and the Pennsylvanians and the host of "Pleasure Time" was underwriting a first-class trip to New York for all eight finalists in his contest, and the glee clubs truly were representative of the whole country. Purdue's competition would come from Dartmouth College, the University of Oklahoma, Elmhurst College (Illinois), Washington and Lee University, Duke University, the University of Redlands (California), and the University of Rochester.

Waring had announced the competition on his radio show in early 1942, stating his intention to find the best college glee club in America. The contest was open to any school, and Waring's representatives had fanned out across the country, listening to the entrants and making recordings for further study. The groups were evaluated on their performance of two songs. "All Through the Night" was required of all competitors, and each could select its own second number.

When Paul Owen, Waring's representative for the Purdue region, arrived in West Lafayette, Al Stewart had chosen "Thanks Be to God" for the optional song, and Owen told the singers he thought they had an excellent chance to make the finals of the competition. Stewart, the son of a Methodist minister, had a deep appreciation for religious music, but he also liked popular songs. He selected his music not for his singers, not for critics, not for himself, but for whatever audience was present, and he was a master at sensing what would make an audience respond.

Official word arrived via telegram from Waring in April: "Confirming last night's radio announcement, Purdue University has won the regional championship in the "Pleasure Time" national glee club competition... Am looking forward to meeting you each personally in New York. Travel details later..." After that, the long practice sessions flew by, and no matter what their director demanded of them, they gave willingly. The Glee Club, in the form they knew it, had existed for barely a decade, and Al Stewart had built it from virtually nothing to this sudden recognition as one of the finest singing groups in the country.

Theirs would be the last "typical" college class of the first half of the twentieth century. America already was at war with the Axis powers. Only because the Selective Service bureaucracy was taking some time gathering speed were most of the young men still in college. Most would serve in the military before the war was over. Frank Onco would be killed in action. Marvin

The 1940 Glee Club. Some of this group would sing at Carnegie Hall in 1942. Many of them would fight in World War II.

President Edward C. Elliott assisted with the Glee Club's send-off at the train station in Lafayette, as the group went off to conquer New York show business in 1942.

Young singers in New York for Fred Waring's national glee club sing-off rehearsed every chance they got. This group burst into song at a Manhattan hotel.

Following the national glee club competition, a gathering of the college men turned into a songfest, which CBS carried in an impromptu late-night broadcast. Fred Waring, in a white dinner jacket, is just below the American flag.

Smith would fly thirty-five missions over Germany in B-24 Liberators. Many would distinguish themselves in their careers. Dick Kohls would become the dean of agriculture at Purdue. Frank Hopf would be one of the most influential dentists in New York State. Jack Silvers would help build the power plant for the USS Nautilus, the world's first nuclear-powered submarine. Although he could not earn a single academic credit for music at Purdue, Art Jacklin would earn a master's degree in music from a prestigious conservatory in Florence, Italy. And Bill Kennedy, with only the Glee Club and his self-administered training in his musical background, would have a singing career that included network radio performances.

Kennedy was one of many students who got through Purdue in part because of the hospitality of Al Stewart and his wife, Charlotte. Arriving on campus with $10 and a beautiful baritone voice as his only assets, Kennedy got a part-time job cataloguing music for the Purdue Musical Organizations. When the Glee Club director heard him sing, Kennedy got both a place in the chorus and a room at the Stewarts' home, where he did odd jobs and ate at the family table. Ultimately Kennedy would get his degree in engineering. Al Stewart had known the same kind of poverty as a college student, and a benefactor had helped him through the hard times. Giving a young man a break was, for Stewart, a natural occurrence in a cycle of charity, and it didn't hurt at all that Kennedy was a great addition to the Glee Club.

Spotting talent and commitment was one of the keys to Stewart's success. In Marvin Smith, he had found one of three Lafayette, Indiana, brothers who would sing for the Glee Club. Marvin, like his older brother, George, had a glorious, clear tenor and so much determination that later, when he was turned down by the Army Air Corps because he missed the five-foot-four-inch minimum height by an inch, he would hang on a stretching contraption at Lambert Fieldhouse until he made the grade with a half-inch to spare. One of his show-stopping numbers was "O Holy Night," sung at the annual Christmas Show of Purdue Musical Organizations. When the star tenor went off to war, Stewart gave the solo to Marvin's eleven-year-old brother, Dick. Al Stewart was a showman.

En route to New York, the Purdue entourage, which included alumni secretary Ethridge B. Baugh, traveled to Indianapolis where they caught the Southwestern Limited for New York. In Cleveland they met up with the Oklahoma glee club. The Sooner singers were wearing buttons that read O.U. Kids.

More than three hundred singers massed Friday afternoon on the steps of New York's city hall where they sang to and were addressed by various dignitaries, including Mayor Fiorello La Guardia. That night, the collegians were Waring's guests at a radio broadcast and at a stage show which followed. Saturday was spent in rehearsals. Four of the glee clubs—Dartmouth, Oklahoma, Elmhurst, and Washington and Lee—would present their concerts Saturday night. Purdue and the other three would sing at 2:30 p.m. Sunday, and Carnegie Hall, with tickets priced at $1.10 and $2.75, would sell out for both U.S.O. benefit shows.

When they left the stage Sunday afternoon, Al Stewart thought they had it won. The Purdue boys had sung magnificently, and there was no question about the audience's choice. When Marvin Smith sang "The White Cliffs of Dover," the people refused to stop applauding until Fred Waring walked onstage and asked for quiet so that the show could continue. It was glorious. But when the results were announced at a banquet that night, Purdue was the runner-up to the University of Rochester Glee Club. The winners, made up of students from Rochester's prestigious Eastman School of Music, had presented a program that was musically more complex than Purdue's. While they hadn't grabbed the audience and shaken it as the Boilermaker troupe had, they had been impressive enough to come out ahead in close balloting.

Although the Rochester group had won, Purdue and Oklahoma were asked to stay Monday night for an appearance on "Pleasure Time" and dinner at the elite Lambs' Club. After the broadcast, the New York visit had a fairytale ending for two of the singers. Bob Wilson, whose father had traveled from Indianapolis for the concert, told Marvin Smith that his family had a table reserved at the Waldorf Astoria's Starlight Room. "If you can get us dates," Wilson said, "the evening is on me." He had asked the right man. That night, Smith and Wilson danced to the music of Tommy Dorsey with Donna Dae and Jean Wilson, two of Fred Waring's singers. The next day, the Glee Club

UNITED STATES MARINES

With the Atlantic Fleet
June, 1942

Dear Mr Stewart,

It's been many months since I've had contact with anything so peaceful as a memory of Purdue, but during one of my few moments of radio listening last Monday night I heard your voice and your glee club's performing for Chesterfield's program.

Two other Purdue men are on this duty tour with me and we all three wish to thank you for a lovely memory recapitulation and congrats on your club's honors.

Sincerely,
Lt J. P. Dolan
U. S. M. C.
Purdue '41

July 23, 1942

Mr. Albert P. Stewart, Dir.,
Men's Glee Club,
Purdue University,
Lafayette, Ind.

Dear Mr. Stewart:

      The Pleasure Time National Glee Club Competition was a source of tremendous satisfaction to me - because it represented the fulfilment of a life-long desire to stimulate interest in collegiate group singing. I honestly believe that the competition did this on a scale never before accomplished.

      In sincere appreciation of your Club's part in the whole project, I am sending along a group of our arrangements which I believe will prove of added interest and value to your repertoire. I hope you will use and enjoy them.

      With my best wishes and the deep conviction that, win or lose, "The Song is the Thing", I am,

Cordially,

Fred Waring
FRED WARING

FW/eh

returned in triumph to the Hoosier State. They had put Purdue on the map. More than forty years later, Smith could say with conviction what everyone ever associated with music at Purdue has accepted: "There is not the shadow of a doubt that the New York trip *made* the Purdue Glee Club. If we could crack New York, we could do anything."

If P.M.O. were to create its own calendar, that trip to New York would separate its eras as emphatically as the birth of Christ divides the history of man. Before that concert in Carnegie Hall, the Purdue Glee Club had been a pleasant campus diversion, a group of clean-cut young men who sounded good and represented the university well around the state. But what did Purdue know about music? This was engineer and farmer country—Silo Tech. The university didn't even teach music. You probably didn't have to go any further than DePauw University, just down Route 231, to hear better singers—at least they had a music school. And down in Bloomington, Indiana University had a hell of a music school. So Al Stewart could talk all he wanted about No Fun without Music and No Music without Fun, but it would never amount to anything but a hobby at Purdue.

The New York trip shattered that logic like a hammer striking a fun-house mirror. The Glee Club had competed with the best groups of its kind in a national arena, and it hadn't merely acquitted itself without embarrassment. It had been terrific. Maybe Al Stewart knew what he was talking about after all.

Facing page: (*Left*) When the Glee Club performed on Fred Waring's program, Purdue graduates already were fighting overseas, and some of them were inspired when they heard the radio broadcast, as this letter indicates. (*Right*) This letter from Fred Waring acknowledged Purdue's part in making the national singing competition a success.

Chapter 2

As a young man, Al Stewart earned a local reputation for having a great voice, a strong presence in theatrical productions, and poise in the limelight.

THE PREACHER'S SON

Albert Pearson Stewart grew up the son of a minister. That fact would influence him all his life, and it would have profound effects on thousands of Purdue University students. Although he didn't follow the religious calling himself and, in fact, was only a teenager when his father died, young Al must have inherited or assimilated a great deal of the spiritual energy and righteous commitment that drove Olin Scott Stewart. Al built his musical organizations around a purposefulness that had an evangelical ring to it, and perhaps this was the most important thing he learned from his father—although he learned a great deal more.

When his second son was born in 1907, Olin Stewart was still trying to launch his ministerial career. To support his family, he was teaching at the one-room Mill School, just south of the turnoff to the Trails at Battle Ground, Indiana. He also was completing his studies at Valparaiso University and being tutored by a Battle Ground minister.

The Reverend Albert L. Miller was responsible for the spiritual welfare of the Methodist people of his community, and he liked having young Olin Stewart around to help with the operation of the Battle Ground Methodist Church. Besides being intelligent and energetic, the aspiring minister liked—and was talented in—music, so Miller put him in charge of the choir.

As a gesture of fellowship—perhaps also as a bit of grandstanding in the interests of good leadership—Olin asked the members of the choir to name his new son. The group decided the name should honor their minister, so the boy became Albert. His mother had been born Ethel Pearson, and baby Al got his middle name from her family.

It should surprise no one that Al Stewart was named by a group of singers. The choice of a namesake, although it seemed whimsical at the time, was to be important in later years. The Reverend Albert L. Miller took the responsibility quite seriously, and his interest in young Albert Stewart would converge with later events and help to shape a destiny. The decision of the church choir was the first of a series of seemingly unrelated events that ultimately would conspire to put Al Stewart on the stage at Purdue for forty years.

After his birth in the 1400 block of Center Street in Lafayette, Al moved with his family to a succession of small towns in the area—Pence, Montmorenci, Waveland—as Olin Stewart's vocation brought new assignments. Olin was not only a popular minister but a community leader, and the growing boy was dedicated to the charismatic father. Decades later, Al would recall Olin this way:

> I remember my dad well. He was a handsome man, tall and slender, with black hair which waved down over his forehead. He was a real community leader and a very popular minister. He played the male roles in all the musicals in community theater groups. Had a fine baritone voice—very dramatic. During the First World War, he was a captain of the Home Guards and did much for all the sick people during the influenza epidemic of 1918. He kept a long list of people he visited regularly so he could give them medicine.

Olin looked after his own interests, too. He supplemented his modest ministerial income with ownership of a grain elevator in Waveland, Indiana. One of the reasons for his popularity as a minister was that he let the showman side of his personality into the church on Sundays. His sermons relied on dramatic impact as well as scriptural substance, and he never forgot how to be a choir director. He put plenty of music into his services, and that was why Al loved them.

It was fortunate for the boy that he liked going to church, because as the preacher's son, he had no choice in the matter: The family was expected to be present at every service, usually four to six of them a week. As living examples to the rest of the flock, the Stewart boys walked a narrow path, or they paid a price. "I'm not sure we were always our dad's pride and joy," Al recalled. "We were embarrassed more than once by the minister telling us from the pulpit to straighten up. When he had to do that before the congregation, he whipped our tails when he got us home."

Still, church was fun for Al because of the music. Olin knew how to get the congregation to belt out a song, and he didn't mind taking a solo himself once in a while. Al loved to sit in the front row watching and listening to his father work the special magic of music on people. The fervent voices would wash around the boy, and he would sing along. Being the showman that he was, Olin knew that nobody can steal a show like a precocious child, so when Al, while still a toddler, began demonstrating a knowledge of melody and lyrics, Olin brought him to the pulpit for an occasional solo. These appearances must have amounted to ecclesiastical novelty numbers for the parishioners, but for the little boy, they were the first delicious taste of the spotlight.

In those days, the Anti-Saloon League was a gathering force, soon to have enough strength to help launch the noble experiment of national Prohibition. The traditional Protestant churches were solidly behind the league, and the crusade against alcohol supplied the inspiration for many a hymn. One of these would become Al Stewart's first hit. It was an old-timey diatribe against the evils of beer. With a boost up to the pulpit from his father, little Al would sing:

> Oh, the brewers' big horses
> Comin' down the road
> Totin' all around their Lucifer's load.
> O, they step so high
> And they step so free
> But the brewers' big horses
> Can't run over me.
> Oh, no boys—Oh, no!
> The turnpike's free
> Wherever I go.
> I'm a toot-toot, choo-choo
> Don't you see.—
> And the brewers' big horses
> Can't run over me.

The congregation loved it, and it would make a neat package to be able to say that the resolve to make music all his life was born then in Al Stewart, but nothing so dramatic happened. To the little boy, singing was just fun and a way to get attention. But the keen and impressionable mind of a child could not have failed to observe the effect of music on those churchgoers. During the group singing, their spirits were lifted, their tensions were released, and they paid tribute to their God. They also had a hell of a good time. Neither could Al have forgotten the feeling that came from being the center of a congregation's attention. With everybody watching and listening to him, he could make a crowd feel what he felt in the music. That was interesting and challenging.

The Stewart family was living in Waveland in 1921, and prospects for the future looked bright. As a small-town minister, Olin would never be wealthy, but he was good at his work and popular with his people. There were four sons now. Glenn was the oldest. After Al had come Delmar and Austin. All were healthy and no more trouble than you would expect boys to be.

Tragedy struck right after Christmas of 1921. The day after the holiday, Olin told his family he was going to Methodist Hospital in Indianapolis for a checkup. There had been no warning of any illness for the rest of the family, but Olin must have been aware of symptoms. Five weeks later, he died of stomach cancer. He was just thirty-nine. When their father died, Al was fifteen, two years younger than Glenn. Delmar was eleven, and Austin was five.

Ethel Stewart was a strong woman and a loving mother, but life would never be easy for her and her four sons without a man in the house. The family would be respectable but poor throughout the rest of Al's youth. Lean times would persist for him well into adulthood.

After Olin's death, Ethel got together what capital she could. She sold the grain elevator and the home in Waveland and bought a house in West Lafayette at 230 Pierce Street. The place was large enough that the family could rent out rooms to a few students. Al remembered his mother's long struggle:

> Mother did a miraculous job of holding us together, and she did it pretty much on a hand-to-mouth basis—borrowing, trading houses, worry-

The Stewart family in 1940. (*From left to right*) Glenn, Austin, Ethel, Delmar, and Al.

The Reverend Olin Scott Stewart.

ing and trying every conceivable thing to keep us fed, clothed and part of a highly respected, though poor, family. I often went for two or three days without one cent in my pocket. That was just the way it was.

Sometimes a nickel would buy me a hot dog or an ice cream cone or a Hershey Bar. On a Saturday afternoon, I might get in to see the *Perils of Pauline*. It is easier for kids today to get dope or alcohol or sex than it was for me to get a candy bar. We got along most of the time by sharing everything. If there was a decent shirt, it was worn by whoever needed it and who got it first. There was no such thing as Al's clothes or Glenn's. They were just our clothes.

Although she never worked at a job other than maintaining her rental rooms, Ethel was determined that her sons wouldn't be deprived of the things their peers enjoyed. "I don't know where the money came from sometimes," Al said. "When one of us talked about having to have something, she'd make sure it was really important, then a few days later, there it would be."

One of the "musts" on Ethel's list was piano lessons for Al. He had begun studying at age nine, and his mother made sure he stayed with it for fifteen years, although he was a reluctant student at times. Like any boy, he could find better things to do than practice the piano when neighborhood play was in full swing. Peer pressure also was a negative influence at times. On one occasion, Ethel enraged her son by buying him a rolled piano music holder instead of the flat one he wanted. "I didn't care anything about the holder, as such," he explained. "I could slide the flat one under my shirt, and nobody could see it while I walked to my lesson. That way, the other boys wouldn't know where I was going, and they wouldn't tease me about having to do sissy stuff."

Al never became what he considered a good pianist, although he could play adequate accompaniment and had a large repertoire. He simply liked voice better, and that was where he directed his energies. However, few people who heard his piano work were as critical of it as he was himself.

Besides the normal boyhood activities and his music lessons, Al found plenty of activities provided through the church. As a minister's son, he spent his summers at the church camps in Battle Ground. There was plenty of camaraderie for youngsters at these gatherings, along with large doses of prayer, testament and spiritual music. Singing evangelists were a regular feature at the camps. Besides their own numbers, these men led the assembled families in group sings, and love of spiritual music sank as deeply into Al Stewart's soul as the religious message the songs carried. Throughout his life, sacred music sung by mixed voices remained his favorite, although it wasn't what made him famous. As an entertainer, he would later recognize the popular appeal of a versatile, all-male group, and he would defer to his audience.

At the camp meetings, there usually was an inspirational service, complete with lots of old-fashioned soul-saving. When members of the assembled flock made their way "down the cinder path" to attest to their acceptance of Jesus as their savior, Al often was right there among them, swearing his commitment to a lifetime of service to the church, weeping with the other sinners and singing hymns with the loudest. "I would cry a little and carry on like everybody else. I was convinced I was doing exactly what I needed to do to please God. I guess I was really preparing for what I ended up doing at Purdue, but I didn't know it."

As her boys got older, Ethel Stewart had all the justification she needed for removing them from school and sending them to work, if not to help support the family, at least to support themselves. But she refused to exercise that option. Her sons had to finish high school, and she wanted them to go to college. That was one reason for living in West Lafayette. As a state school, Purdue was the easiest to manage financially.

As a student at West Lafayette High School, Al worked at odd jobs in order to help out at home. Starting when he was sixteen, he worked at the Luna Theater, where he was the "relief girl" for the ticket seller, who took her dinner break every afternoon from 4:30 until 6:45. He also ushered at the movie house and learned to love the silent films of the 1920s. The theater job brought in a little money, and it allowed Al to be in on exciting events, such as the opening of Al Jolson's revolutionary movie *The Jazz Singer*, the first talkie. As movie sound tracks improved, Al developed a love of the Nelson Eddy-Jeanette MacDonald romances, some of which he saw seven or eight times. Al understood not only the appeal of their music, but the vocal techniques they and the chorus accompaniment used. "I watched every minute of every one of those films," he could report. "I liked it and I learned."

But there was a more important fringe benefit of the Luna job. Because of the work, Al developed connections with everyone in town who had anything to do with show business. This was the beginning of a personal network that would extend someday throughout the United States and across two oceans to include some of the most famous entertainers in the world. In the beginning, though, Al's connections just got him walk-on and chorus parts in some of the live shows that were put on at the Mars Theater on Sixth Street in Lafayette.

The Mars had opened in 1921 with a show that starred Ed Wynn—not yet known as the Texaco Fire Chief, but famous as a stage comedian. The Mars was the only theater in town equipped to handle a professional stage show. It remained the premier showcase in the Lafayette area until Purdue's Hall of Music opened its doors in 1941.

As a tall, handsome youngster with a strong presence and the growing polish he was picking up in his theater associations, Al stood out from the other teenagers. He was a fixture in music programs at West Lafayette High School, where he performed in a string of the operettas that were popular in the 1920s. At the First Methodist Church, he sang in a choir that was several cuts above other local groups. Its director, Paul T. Smith, was a professor of history at Purdue, where he also directed the Men's Glee Club.

The early exposure to music, his training, his talent and the unusual amount of experience he was picking up earned Al a local reputation and made him an excellent prospect for Smith's singing group at Purdue. After Al's senior year at West Lafayette High, he received a letter from Smith, welcoming him into the Purdue Glee Club. This may have been a subtle recruiting device, as well as a friendly gesture. In either case, it made a powerful impression on the boy. Years later Al remembered it, and in typical Stewart fashion, he added his own twist by establishing the practice of writing similar letters to the newborn babies of Glee Club alumni. In the course of years, the letters began coming back to Al—at P.M.O. auditions in the hands of the now-grown babies who had received them. The parents of those infants religiously tucked them away, then brought them out as their children reached high-school age.

Chapter 3

After graduating from high school, Al attended Purdue part-time for a year. He probably passed Eliza Fowler Hall daily, little dreaming that just a few years later he would be given that building by President Elliott to house the growing musical organizations.

INTERLUDE AT PURDUE

When Smith sent his letter in 1927, there seemed no doubt that Al would be singing in the Purdue Glee Club in a matter of months. Smith had recognized the boy's ability; Al was eager to sing under someone he recognized as an excellent and dynamic director; and, anyway, no other university was in financial reach for the fatherless Stewart family. But for the second time, an untimely death jolted Al's life. Paul Smith died of a ruptured appendix before his protégé finished high school. Suddenly, Al's resolve to start college was not so keen.

If Al Stewart's adult life had been troubled or marred by failure, it would be easy and natural to point to the unexpected deaths of two important father figures as the source of his problems. The fact that he enjoyed stability and success that belie his modest beginnings may have been despite the early tragedies, or these losses may have hardened the steel within. The man who lost a father and then an idol during impressionable times of his youth became a demanding, often stern, father figure to thousands of young people. Somehow, the chemistry was just right for Stewart and Purdue when the two came together.

But at the time of Smith's death, the attraction of Purdue was far from irresistible. Al had found more satisfaction in music than anything else, and it certainly was something he did well, but he hadn't made plans for a career as a musician, a singer or a music teacher. He had rather lukewarm intentions about studying psychology or sociology at Purdue, but he was viewing the prospect of academics at the university as little more than a necessary evil that would allow him to sing for Paul Smith. A college degree would enhance his career possibilities, but he still had no idea what that career would be, so there was no hurry.

After his mentor's death, Stewart gave in to the severe financial pressures that continued to beset his family. He decided to postpone his education so that he could earn some money to help his mother. He kept the part-time job at the theater after graduating from high school, and he picked up whatever work came his way. He pumped gas at a Shell station. He sold shoes. He waited on tables. He cut grass. But he also kept singing and performing in local productions and in church.

Two years after finishing high school, with his brother Glenn now out of college and working, Al finally enrolled at Purdue as a social sciences major. His entry was a comparatively triumphant one for a freshman, because he arrived as the star-designate of a musical production that had been written specifically for his talents. Through his work at the Mars Theater, Al had become friends with Floyd Kendall, who played the pipe organ at the playhouse. Kendall was an enormously talented man, who could play almost any musical work in any key after hearing it once. He had a huge repertoire and wrote his own music, as well. In Al's memory, "Floyd was amazing. He could be playing a difficult piece and be reading a newspaper or giving someone directions to a certain restaurant without ever missing a note. The music just seemed to come out of his fingers." Two decades later, Al would discover a comparable gift in a Purdue freshman named Bill Luhman, and he would instantly know the value of that gift.

Kendall's talents did not go unappreciated at the Mars. He was one of the best-paid men in town at $100 a week, and his dapper wardrobe advertised his status. He also had an eye for show business potential, and he thought he saw some in young Al Stewart. An annual activity at Purdue was an all-male musical review, which was staged at the Mars. Kendall was engaged to write the show for the fall of 1928, and he let it be known that he was writing it for Al Stewart, who would be enrolling in the fall.

The production, called *Ad Noise*, was a musical satire of the advertising business. Before Al took his first class at the university, he had the entire score and script down cold. There was little chance of anyone else beating out the brash freshman for the lead role. *Ad Noise* became a local hit show that year, and Al became a campus celebrity.

The "leading lady" in that production of *Ad Noise* was Kenny Gano, a boy from the New York City area. His mother was with the Metropolitan Opera Ballet, where she taught dance. A French woman with a limited command of the English language but with vast experience in life, she had trained her son in dancing and the theater arts, and Kenny made a convincing girl. "He had these beautifully proportioned muscular legs, and he could walk and move exactly like a young woman," Al recalls. "But he was anything but a sissy. He was a terrific wrestler, as well as a good dancer. He had been around show business so long that it all came easy for him, and pretending to be a girl didn't bother him like it would have some of us."

When the show opened, Madame Gano came from New York to watch her son's debut at Purdue. Stewart and Gano shared a dressing room at the Mars, and when Al arrived on opening night, Kenny was there, and his mother was with him, helping him get into the padding and makeup he needed to become a believable female. Al waited anxiously as the Ganos matter-of-factly assembled Kenny's costume. The clock ticked relentlessly toward curtain time. Finally Madame Gano noticed the leading man's inactivity. "Are you not going to dress, my boy?" she asked.

"Uh, yes, ma'am," Al said, but he made no move.

"Then why not you dress?" she persisted. "Oh, oh! I see now. You think I should leave. My dear boy, I have been in the theater all my life. If you have something I have not seen, please—show it to me!"

It was that night that Al realized there was a big world outside Lafayette and that not everyone in that world had grown up in a Methodist parsonage.

If Al's first year at Purdue started with a bang, it ended with a whimper. He enjoyed campus life and sang in the Glee Club, which now was directed by Helen Faust Smith, the widow of Paul, but Al had little enthusiasm for his studies. For music, he had a passion, but to social sciences he was indifferent. By the end of the school year, he was in academic trouble, and he decided to withdraw from Purdue to take a job with the Lafayette Life Insurance Company.

Failure to make good grades that year contributed to what Al thinks is a record for wearing a fraternity pledge pin. He had pledged Delta Upsilon while a sophomore at West Lafayette High. This was a common practice at the time. "We had to wear our pledge pins backwards with the pin inside the shirt and the little stud facing out, but we were considered pledges and had the run of the fraternity house," he said. "When I didn't start at Purdue right out of high school, I still was a pledge, since I knew I'd enroll eventually. But then I didn't make my grades that first year, so I couldn't be initiated. When I finally got into the fraternity, I was at DePauw, and I'd had that pin for seven years." Except for one night when Al nearly severed his tie with *DU*. By his own analysis, Al was pretty cocky for a freshman. His notoriety because of the show, his comparatively advanced age and his high opinion of himself caused some of the fraternity's brothers to conclude that he was getting too big for his britches; and one night they told him so. Because of the expense, Al didn't live in the *DU* house. He ate dinner there regularly and slept at home. When the fraternity's members confronted him after dinner, Al was unrepentant: "I took off the pin and threw it down, and told them I didn't need their fraternity. Then I walked out. The next morning about ten of them were on my porch, wanting to take me to breakfast and talk about it. They were right in bringing me up short. I *was* pretty cocky, and I behaved myself a little better after that."

The job with Lafayette Life Insurance provided some money, but very little satisfaction for Al. The work required him to keep track of the accounts, which meant a large daily dose of applied mathematics, a science for which he had little aptitude and even less interest. However, he needed the job, and he worked hard enough to hold onto the position through the summer and fall of 1929. Meanwhile, he enrolled part-time at Purdue, with the intention of going back as soon as he could.

During his year at Purdue, Al had organized a dance band, which he called Al Stewart's Campus Commanders. In the tradition of small-town dance bands everywhere, the Campus Commanders played anywhere they could get a job, provided they could reach it by car. The band's sound filled the Purdue Memorial Union regularly on weekends, and Al got bookings at the Michigan lake resorts, as well as at clubs and road houses in the Lafayette area. The fourteen-piece group played the popular dance tunes of the day in the big-band style popularized by Paul Whiteman. Al directed, did most of the vocals and handled the bookings.

"It was a good way to make some money," he said, "and it was a good band. I had a fine guitar player and a first-rate drummer. Of course they all thought they were vocalists. They could talk so they thought they could sing."

During the summer, he booked the Commanders into the Sportsman Hotel on Lake Freeman in Monticello, Indiana, for the entire resort season. The catch was that the band's income was based on a percentage of the hotel's profits, which weren't very much during those hard times. "It was a pathetic thing sometimes," Al said. "We'd play every night, and sometimes there wouldn't be ten people in the place. But there was an old house across the street, and they let us stay there, and we all got to eat at the Sportsman for free."

This was actually a pretty good deal for the time. Al could croon "My Blue Heaven," and the Commanders could belt out "Yessir, That's My Baby," knowing that they'd be able to order breakfast in the morning. A lot of Americans didn't have as strong a guarantee on the source of their next meal.

However, the local musicians union didn't think as much of the arrangement. At the end of the summer, the organization slapped the leader of Al Stewart's Campus Commanders with a $100 fine for booking a job at less than the union scale. Al was bitter about the penalty. "I managed to keep fourteen guys working and fed with a roof over their heads all summer when there were no jobs around, and for my trouble I got to pay a fine."

Besides the Commanders, Al had a smaller "society band," a five-piece ensemble that played regularly at luncheon events in the Purdue Union, among other places, but his musical enterprises were a form of moonlighting and amusement. His "real" job was still with Lafayette Life, where he reported every morning to work his way through the columns of figures. Early in the fall, he was given a short vacation, and he decided to use it to visit his brother Glenn. After graduating from Purdue, Glenn had gone to work for Commercial Solvents Company in Terre Haute. A bus ride from Lafayette to Terre Haute meant a trip to Crawfordsville, then a transfer to another bus for the second leg of the journey. Al's bus out of Lafayette was late, so he missed the transfer. This left him with three hours to kill in Crawfordsville, so he decided to take a walking tour of Wabash College, which he had never seen.

The little Crawfordsville college still was an important rival of Purdue's in those days. It had been just a few years since Wabash students had applied the nickname Boilermakers to Purdue athletic teams as a scornful reference to the university's alleged recruitment of burly laborers for its football squads. The two schools had continued to compete on the gridiron until 1928, when Purdue's growth and movement into national sports prominence made the rivalry too one-sided.

An indifferent fate occasionally seems to take a brief, whimsical interest in certain mortals. These flashes of fortune often create small turning points that lead to major changes in our destinies, and one of them happened to Al Stewart on that day in Crawfordsville, Indiana. After walking around the campus for a short time, he started back to the bus station when he passed the Trinity Methodist Church. Behind the church was the parsonage, and on the rear building a sign. It read: The Reverend Albert L. Miller, Pastor.

Al had not seen or thought about the Reverend Albert L. Miller for a long time, but he knew his namesake well, both by reputation and because of the family friendship that had endured through the years since Olin Stewart had assisted at Miller's Battle Ground church. It was about five in the afternoon when Al walked past the Crawfordsville parsonage, and he still had some time before the next bus to Terre Haute. "I thought it would be kind of fun to say hello and see if he remembered that I was named after him."

Miller not only remembered, he had taken steps that very day that would help determine Al's future. When he saw the young man on his doorstep that afternoon, he gaped as though he had seen an apparition. As Al remembered their reunion, Miller said, "I can't believe this. I was on the telephone just this afternoon, talking to Dean McCutcheon about you. I was planning to try to get in touch with you this evening. I've got a proposition for you."

That summer, Al had sung the baritone lead in an outdoor production of Dubois's "The Seven Last Words of Christ" at Battle Ground. Among the 1,500 people in the audience was Albert L. Miller. He was impressed with the

VII. MEMOIRS

A. MINISTERS

ALBERT L. MILLER

Albert L. Miller, the son of Robert E. and Jane Burton Miller, was born December 27, 1867, near Harriettsville, Ohio. During his young manhood he taught school and attended West Farmington College in northeastern Ohio, where he graduated in 1895. The year before his graduation he was married to Lyda Danford, of near Caldwell, Ohio, who was a student at the same college.

Upon graduation from college he took his first charge in the Northwest Indiana Conference. He served the following churches: Burnettsville, Richland Center, New Carlisle, Battle Ground, Congress Street, Lafayette, Danville, Rossville, Remington, Oxford, Trinity, Crawfordsville, Flora, Jamestown, and Darlington, in all totaling 44 years in the active ministry.

Rev. Mr. Miller's wife passed away on May 30, 1928, while he was pastor in Crawfordsville and his niece, Josephine A. Miller, came to take charge of his household throughout the rest of his ministry and during his retirement years, assisting him with his work, and serving faithfully in the churches where he was pastor.

Brother Miller was ever busy about the Lord's work even when he was in his retirement years. During the war years, when many ministers were in service, he did much supply work, serving regularly at Yountsville and Kirkpatrick. He assumed various duties connected with the church and was always ready to help where needed. For the six years preceeding his death he was financial secretary for the Darlington church. He loved his work as a minister and often encouraged the younger men in their work or led young men to make the ministry their life work. He believed in and taught the eternal goodness of God.

Brother Miller passed to his heavenly reward on Tuesday, December 19, 1950, after having been in failing health for two years, but never confined to his bed until just a day before his death. Funeral services were held on Friday afternoon at 2 o'clock from the Methodist church in Darlington, with the Reverend Elmer Jones, superintendent of the Crawfordsville District officiating, having the assistance of the Rev. Thomas L. Stovall, of Terre Haute, a former pastor at Darlington. He was laid to rest in Grandview Cemetery at West Lafayette, Indiana.

Albert L. Miller

This memoir from a religious publication tells of Albert Miller's devotion to his profession. He was also dedicated to helping his young namesake, Al Stewart, get an education in music at DePauw.

The Trinity Methodist Church of Crawfordsville, where the Reverend Albert L. Miller was pastor in 1929. Photo and memoir courtesy of Trinity United Methodist Church, 110 South Blair Street, Crawfordsville.

singing ability and the presence of his young namesake, and he concluded that it was his duty to see to it that such talent had the opportunity to develop. Knowing that formal music training was not available at Purdue and that Al was far too advanced for any local instructors to help him, Miller had called Dean Robert G. McCutcheon at the DePauw University Music School in Greencastle. Miller described the talents, the good family background and the lean financial circumstances of his protégé and suggested that McCutcheon could help a promising young man and add a fine voice to DePauw's choir by granting Al a scholarship to the music school. Miller was prepared to pay Al's living expenses at DePauw if the scholarship were granted.

McCutcheon, it turned out, also had heard Stewart sing, and he agreed that the young baritone would make a good addition to the school. And so the bargain was struck that afternoon without consultation with Al Stewart, who was riding the bus from Lafayette to Crawfordsville while his two benefactors plotted out his future. When Miller had outlined the proposition to him that afternoon, Al was enthusiastic about the scholarship and the possibility for a real education in music, but he wasn't prepared to accept the offer on the spot. His first obligation was to his mother, who still was raising two young boys in Lafayette. The only way Al felt he could leave was if he could persuade his older brother, Glenn, to return to Lafayette. Glenn's job was in Terre Haute, but Al had an idea.

His mind whirling with plans, he couldn't even wait for the bus to Terre Haute. Instead, he rushed out to Route 231 and started thumbing his way south. Hope and fear took turns dominating his thoughts as he traveled. The plan was beautiful in its simplicity: Al could go to DePauw if brother Glenn would leave his position in Terre Haute and take over Al's job at Lafayette Life. Not only would Ethel Stewart have one of her grown sons home to be the man of the house, but Al could leave the hated mathematics behind for a life full of music. Of course, Glenn had to agree to the arrangement. The other potential problem was Lafayette Life. Fred Alexander, the president of the company, wasn't accustomed to trading junior office workers like utility infielders, but when Al, having gotten Glenn's approval for the scheme, explained the plan and all its ramifications, Alexander accepted the exchange.

The "Stewart switch" turned out to be an even neater package than Al had envisioned. His supervisor in the insurance office had been a pretty Lafayette girl named Lillian Balkema. It didn't take Glenn long to notice her and vice versa. The two began a courtship that led to marriage, and Glenn succeeded Lillian in her job. Before he retired from the company nearly four decades later, he had risen to vice president and secretary of Lafayette Life and was a member of the board of directors. So Al Stewart's life was only one of many changed forever by a bus to Crawfordsville that missed its connection.

Going to DePauw, of course, meant severing ties with Purdue, and Al met some resistance from one of the university's deans. Richard Moore was dean of science, and he had some strong reservations about Al's decision to attend another university. Al always blamed this opposition on the dean's reluctance to lose a young celebrity to another school. After all, the star of *Ad Noise* and the leader of the Campus Commanders—despite his academic shortcomings—had made a name for himself. However, Moore, in confronting Al, based his arguments on the uncertainties of music as a career foundation.

"Just what do you expect to do?" he asked. "Do you think you have enough voice to become an opera star?"

No. Young Stewart didn't honestly think he did.

"Do you intend to teach public school?"

"God forbid! I couldn't stand that."

"Well, just what *are* you going to do with this education, which can't earn you a living and which you can't afford?"

Al considered the challenge for only a second before answering: "You know, I don't have any idea except for one thing. I have a very strong personal feeling that somehow this is what I should do, and that if I go ahead on the basis that this has been worked out so beautifully for me—not my doing—that something will open up and I'll have a decent life."

Moore did not think a career could be built on pipe dreams and a misplaced belief in the favor of destiny. He dismissed the erstwhile student with a strong and gloomy prediction of the failures that awaited under such an ill-considered plan. Dejected, Al trudged over to Salisbury Street to the home of his favorite professor, Dr. Oakel Hall. A lay minister in the Methodist Church,

Hall had a large family and extended his fatherly attitude to his students. When he heard Al's account of the meeting with the dean, Hall grabbed the telephone and called Moore. Discouraging promising young men was not the proper business of educators, Hall said. "Here is a student with desire and a vision of what he wants to do. We should be encouraging him, not running him down."

Hall's phone call meant little in practical terms. The dean couldn't have kept Al at Purdue if he'd wanted to. But the gesture of support came at exactly the right time. "I've always been grateful to Professor Hall, because he gave me a little bit of assurance—a little more feeling for what I wanted to do, and I tried to do the same with students when my time came. I hope I never gave advice—only counseling. When they came to me with a problem about a girlfriend or a career or religion, I tried to get them to listen to their own heart. Youngsters usually must do what they are determined to do, whether or not it makes sense to other people."

Chapter 4

Financial hardship led Al to drop out of DePauw in 1930, but in 1960 the university would recognize his achievements by conferring the honorary degree of Doctor of Music on him.

DOWN AND OUT AT DEPAUW

A l arrived on the DePauw campus in September 1929, full of high hopes, but almost devoid of other resources. He wore his only clothes, a light blue suit with wide white pin stripes. He had bought it on sale for $7 and in his own words, "it really was a mess." All his possessions were in a huge trunk he had bought at a Lafayette secondhand store. Since the lock was broken, the trunk was secured with a length of clothesline rope. This added up to a humble—even a comical—appearance, but things were even worse than they looked, because the trunk—five feet long, four feet wide, four feet deep—was almost empty. Three or four shirts, three or four sets of underwear, some socks and toilet articles made a layer about four inches deep in the bottom of the trunk, which has stayed in the Stewart family ever since, good for a laugh, but also a serious reminder of humble beginnings.

The DePauw experience was a strange combination of success and constant desperation for Al. Albert L. Miller was as good as his word in making sure his protégé's tuition was paid, and a check for living expenses arrived every month. On campus and in the classroom, Al found himself comfortable and confident: "I had had a rough time at Purdue in classwork that I was not particularly well suited for. It was a good feeling to be making good grades in something I really wanted to do and that I thought I had some talent for."

In December of that year, Miller wrote to Al with obvious pride and satisfaction: "So glad to hear from you again, and especially to sense the tone of the letter. It had the *right ring*.

"So glad you are climbing to the top in your grades. Hope you can make straight A in every subject. You know there is no crowding among the high graders in college. You have room for expansion. It will mean so much in later life to have the record of top grades. You have the ability for this. You can do it, I am sure."

Miller's letter went on to congratulate Al for standing out as a vocalist, but applauded his restraint in turning down a chance to become a campus celebrity. The music school at DePauw produced an annual Christmas pageant, and one of Al's professors sang the lead role. Recognizing the need to have a stand-in available in case something prevented him from singing, the professor asked his new pupil—Al Stewart—to learn the part. Miller wrote: "If I were you, I think I would feel just a *Little Puffed*. But no doubt you don't let such things disturb your equilibrium."

The professor was not the only one who had spotted Al's singing and entertaining abilities. An important DePauw event was an annual Revue, put on by student players. The committee responsible for the production approached the freshman from West Lafayette less than three months after he arrived on campus. Would he be interested in the male lead in the Revue that spring? The offer was tempting for several reasons. Starring in the Revue would mean local fame and, even more important, instant acceptance on campus. The doors to other performances would open, and, of course, there was a chance to get on stage. For a born showman like Al Stewart, no appeal could be stronger.

But Al had been there before. He knew that his academic troubles at Purdue had been caused—at least partly—by his preoccupation with the All-Men's Revue production of *Ad Noise*. He decided he needed to get his feet on the ground and his nose into his books before grabbing the brass ring. Albert Miller applauded the decision:

> You were certainly wise to turn down the Revue proposition. It would have meant much hard work, and temporary glory. That kind of work appeals to many people. Just present glory. It may take you a little longer to keep in the regular and sane channel of procedure, but you are getting the foundation for life's work that will endure long after the applause has died away. Your broad musical education will be your capital. With it and your superior ability, you can get all the applause any person needs and

more, you can demand that remuneration that will make you independent. This is no flattery. I would not say it if it were not true. Just keep on increasing your capital, and the interest will take care of itself. See?

That kind of advice, as firm and as tested as the Indiana soil from which it sprang, was a standard enclosure in envelopes which brought Al's monthly checks. The confidence that Miller expressed in the musical talents he had invested in was typical of most of the people who knew the young Al Stewart. In fact, the only person who seemed to have any reservations about that talent was Al himself.

Al Stewart, at age twenty-one, had every excuse for believing he had a remarkable vocal talent. People had been telling him so all his life, beginning when he had sung in his father's church while barely more than a toddler. As he matured, the praise increased, and it came from increasingly sophisticated sources. If Floyd Kendall, who made $100 a week, could write him his own musical, if the DePauw Revue committee wanted him to star, if Rev. Albert L. Miller was willing to invest in him, why should Al doubt his own ability?

Yet he did doubt. More than that, he *knew*, despite what everyone else told him, that there were limits to what he could accomplish as a singer. During a lifetime of achievement in a frequently hostile environment, Al neither earned nor cultivated a reputation for modesty, but he didn't kid himself either. He was always coldly objective when he evaluated a voice, and he didn't flinch from assessing his own as he would anyone else's. Was he perhaps too stringent in judging himself? Could the combination of his voice, his ambition and that extra flair that always seemed to set him apart have been parlayed into a successful career as a vocalist? The question became moot as soon as he made up his mind not to follow that path. The men and women who sang for him throughout the years that followed learned quickly that Al's decisions were final. He had absolute faith in his own judgment, they say. But he had something more than that, something more than plain stubbornness—although he never denied possessing a streak of that valuable commodity. He simply wasn't afraid to be wrong. In the final analysis, that fear is what holds most of us back from the great things each of us knows he is capable of. It wasn't that Al didn't think he could make mistakes; he has admitted to a fair share of them over the years. It was just that once he had made a decision, he put his energy into implementing it, not into worrying whether the decision was right or wrong. Others may have wondered what kind of singing career he might have had, but he never thought about it at all.

Albert Miller's generosity was not enough to free Al from the heavy thumb of the Great Depression. He was successful in the classroom and popular on campus, but having enough to live on and not a penny more was a daily ordeal from which he couldn't escape. The only luxury he permitted himself was membership in his fraternity. He finally took off the seven-year pledge pin and was duly initiated into Delta Upsilon, but he couldn't afford to live in the fraternity house. Instead, he took a room on Hanna Street in Greencastle and walked to the house each day for lunch and dinner. In order to get the money to pay his dues, he skipped breakfast. To a son of Ethel Pearson Stewart, the sacrifice was a small one. It was important to be one of the guys.

One of the best things about DePauw, as far as Al was concerned, was working under Dr. Robert McCutcheon, the dean of the music school. McCutcheon was a dedicated musician who recognized something special in the freshman and constantly challenged him to develop his talents. Al, in turn, saw in McCutcheon the kind of man he could admire and emulate—both personally and professionally. The dean taught him not just music, but also directing skills, stage presence and human relations. McCutcheon had been born with one leg shorter than the other and walked with a pronounced limp. Al modeled his early directing style so closely on McCutcheon's that after directing his first concert at Purdue, he wrote this letter:

> Dear Dean,
> I expect you are quite tired for you've just finished directing your first chorus. Oh I know it was I who was standing up there, but when I closed my eyes I saw myself as Dean McCutcheon and I worked accordingly. The only thing I didn't do that you would have done was limp when I walked off the stage.

Far from being offended by the reference to his handicap, McCutcheon delighted in telling people—especially his students—about the letter.

Robert McCutcheon, music dean at DePauw University when Al Stewart was a student there, had a considerable influence on Al's early directing style.

Under McCutcheon, DePauw had developed a choir that built some regional fame. As a member of the group, Al began to refine his sense of how audiences respond to singers. He also learned something about being on the road with an entertainment ensemble. The choir traveled around the state, usually to sing in churches. The singers usually could expect a ham-and-beans supper in the church basement, and overnight accommodations were offered by parishioners who opened up their homes to the students. There was an auction-block quality to this arrangement. The singers would be brought forward in ones and twos, and the minister or the local choir director would say, "Who will take these two boys?" This system and the awkwardness of being a guest in the homes of strangers embarrassed Al:

> I decided then that if I ever had responsibility for young singers, I would do everything I could to keep them from having to stay in private homes. If I could get enough money from performances, I'd treat them to a hotel whenever we were on the road. It was always hard for us to be "farmed out" the way we were, and I never forgot it. When the Glee Club started traveling extensively, I always put them in good hotels. The only time we made an exception was when we visited Buckeburg, Germany. I wanted the boys to stay in German homes, so they could get to know the people and the culture.

The curriculum and the environment at DePauw were giving Al a strong taste of what a career in music could be like, and he liked the taste very much. Still, the grim business of survival was wearing him down. Other students might stop for a soda after class or treat a girl to a hamburger or a movie, but there was no room in Al's budget for that kind of luxury. His mother couldn't help; there were no jobs to be had, and to ask Albert Miller for more money would sacrifice more pride than Al could spare.

On one particularly dismal morning, he was hungry, completely out of money and drained of spirit. He left the house on Hanna Street to walk to DePauw's administration building and withdraw from school. Two steps from his door he looked down, and there on the sidewalk was a $5 bill. "I had a wonderful breakfast that morning, and my discouragement flew away, for a while at least." But only for as long as $5 could last. By the time classes ended in June of 1930, he had decided that, even with a scholarship and the support of Albert Miller, he couldn't afford to go to college and live on his own. In Lafayette he at least could stay at home, and he might get enough work to support himself. He left DePauw that June with the dream of a degree in music shattered.

Chapter 5

When Charlotte Friend met Al upon his return from DePauw in 1930, she already had established a successful singing career. Until this time, however, Al's life had been defined chiefly by poverty and tragedy. Soon his luck would change and he would begin building a music program at Purdue that would someday gain world prominence. Charlotte is pictured at age twenty-one.

TURNING POINT

The summer of 1930 was not a good one for America, but it was a great one for Al Stewart. The economic chaos that had begun the previous October got worse instead of better; confidence in the government receded faster every day, and men who had proudly supported their families all their lives suddenly found themselves without jobs or dignity; Al's team, the Chicago Cubs, would not successfully defend the National League pennant. But Al's personal slump would end. Life was about to hang him a curve ball, and he was going to hit a home run.

Just a few days after he returned from DePauw, he heard about an ice cream social to be held on the lawn of the Wesley Foundation on State Street in West Lafayette. The First Methodist Church was sponsoring the event as a fund raiser for its choir, and Al thought it would he a good chance to renew old acquaintances. Almost as soon as he arrived, he noticed a very slender, black-haired girl, sitting alone in a corner. He looked around for a familiar face and spotted Kenneth Cohee, an old friend. "Who's the girl in the white dress?" Al asked, after exchanging greetings.

Cohee said her name was Charlotte Friend. Al recognized the name. A nineteen-year-old home economics major at Purdue, Charlotte had developed a local reputation as a fine soprano, and that interested Al almost as much as the fact that she was very pretty and apparently alone. He asked Cohee to introduce him. Al noticed that Charlotte was wearing a Sigma Phi Epsilon fraternity pin, but that didn't stop him from asking if he could walk her home at the end of the evening. She said she was sorry, but she was riding home with Helen Smith, the choir director of First Methodist. To Al, that was not a turndown but a challenge. He quickly located Mrs. Smith and asked, "Helen, could I get a ride home with you?"

"Of course, Al," she said. "But I'm taking Charlotte Friend home, too. I hope you don't mind."

When he arrived home later that night, Al told his older brother about the girl he had met. "Why do you always have to go after something you can't have?" Glenn demanded. "She's pinned to a Sig Ep, and you might as well forget about her." Al replied that he had $10 that said he would have the fraternity pin off before Christmas. He collected on the bet before Purdue resumed classes in September. Charlotte had been pinned to a boy whose family was in the beer business in Kentucky. She planned to give back his pin the day he returned. The couple went to an early evening movie in Lafayette. Al, meanwhile, spent the evening working at the Luna. On the way home, he decided to walk across the river to West Lafayette because he was afraid of running into Charlotte and her ex-beau on the streetcar. Crossing Second Street, though, he decided the odds were against such an encounter, and he got on the next car that stopped. Charlotte and the boy were sitting in a front seat. Al slunk to the rear, triumphant, but embarrassed. Charlotte was his girl from then on.

Charlotte Friend was a member of a large and remarkable family. She, her two sisters and four brothers all would graduate from Purdue; a fifth boy died in infancy. The Friends were a lively group with talent, ambition and sparkle. Charlotte, Josephine and Mary sang together as the Friend Sisters Trio, appearing in local clubs, at festivals and as a specialty group with the Purdue Men's Glee Club and with various other university singing ensembles. They also performed on local radio and made singing commercials for Lafayette merchants, including their own father, for whom they sang the praises of a medicinal ointment he had developed. The girls all had successful careers as soloists, as well. Josephine sang with Lafayette dance bands, chiefly the Bud Bryant Band. Bryant billed her as "the Vest Pocket Venus of Song." Mary starred in numerous productions at Purdue, including the Gilbert and Sullivan operas *H.M.S. Pinafore*, *The Mikado* and *The Pirates of Penzance*.

The Friend brothers also were well known in Lafayette. Lloyd and Ray sang for Al Stewart in the Purdue Musical Organizations. Paul, known as "Dufe," excelled in basketball. The youngest brother, Bob, was not a P.M.O. member or varsity athlete only because his athletic talent overshadowed everything else. It took him eight years to get through Purdue, because he had to alternate his semesters with professional baseball seasons, first as a minor leaguer and eventually as a member of the Pittsburgh Pirates pitching staff. Bob was the workhorse of the Pirates' rotation for sixteen years, including their world championship season in 1960.

The patriarch of the family, R. T. Friend, insisted that all his children have music lessons of some kind, but as a youngster, Bob was indifferent to his mandatory piano lessons. He was constantly sneaking off to play baseball or persuading his older brothers or Al Stewart to catch for him while he refined his pitching skills. Finally R. T. came up with a way to use the boy's passion for baseball as a tool in his musical education. R. T. decreed that the other boys—and Al—could catch for Bob only for the length of time he had practiced piano: an hour at the keyboard, an hour on the mound; no practice, no pitching. Under this system, Bobby became a pretty good piano player and a hell of a pitcher. Al, for whom the Friend house on Maple Street became a second home from the time he began to court Charlotte, learned to dread the sound of the piano. "I knew when I heard it that I'd have to catch Bobby, and was going to end up with a sore hand. Even as a little kid, he threw pretty hard, and he just wore us out."

Al wasn't the only young man to enjoy the hospitality of the big house on Maple. R. T. and his wife, Anna, loved young people, and they loved Purdue. It was this warm affection, rather than polite convention, that governed their life. The mantle in their living room served as a kind of campus bulletin board. Notices of entertainment events, campus meetings, parties, items for sale and roommate needs were posted there and rotated as new ones appeared. A student could always get a meal there. Besides the many bedrooms where family members slept, there was a large second-floor room with an outside entrance—never locked. The room contained several beds, freshly made up

(*Left*) This old family photo shows the patriarch R. T. Friend with three of his children: Mary, Lloyd and Charlotte.

(*Below*) Mrs. Albert P. Stewart was a diminutive soloist with a big voice for the 1933–34 Men's Glee Club.

every day, and any student or guest who needed a place to spend the night could sleep there. Each morning, R. T. would climb the stairway to see who had spent the night in the guest room. Then he'd invite them down to breakfast.

Al and Charlotte were almost inseparable from the day they met, but he felt that her singing ability was too good for her to neglect a formal musical education. DePauw had been too much for him financially, but Charlotte's family could handle it, Al argued. At his urging, she transferred to the Greencastle university, where she spent three semesters as a music major before returning to Purdue to get her degree in home economics in 1933.

Although she was a tiny—almost frail-looking—young woman, Charlotte was possessed of a powerful soprano voice. This contrast gave her an enormously effective stage presence. In Al's words: "Audiences—especially if they'd never heard her before—were just awed to hear these tremendous sounds coming from this little bitty girl. God, she could sing!" Although the visual effect enhanced her talent, Charlotte's voice could stand on its own merits. The number she became most identified with was "Italian Street Song," which allowed an excellent blending of male chorus and soprano. When she sang it with the Purdue Glee Club, the song became an almost tangible force. With the virile men's voices swelling below her, Charlotte would soar effortlessly among the treacherous high notes. Audiences literally held their breath until they erupted in applause at the last note. On one occasion in the late 1930s, Charlotte and the Glee Club performed "Italian Street Song" as the finale of a concert over Chicago radio station WLS. Shortly after they had finished, the station's general manager arrived at the studio, having just driven to work. "I just heard the end of your concert on the radio," he told Al. "My God, what a soprano you have! Who is she?"

Al said, "Thanks, that's my wife."

"Well," the manager grinned, "I'm glad I didn't say she was terrible."

Charlotte was a regular feature with the Glee Club for almost two decades, although after her graduation in 1933, technically she had no affiliation with the university. There were no restrictions against such an arrangement in those days, and with her petite figure and youthful face, Charlotte probably looked, to audiences who didn't know her, like a Purdue coed, even when she was well into her thirties and the mother of two children. Al was happy to keep her singing as long as he could: "We got to spend more time together, and besides, she was damn good."

Spotting the dark-haired girl in the corner at the Methodist ice cream social was a great turning point in Al's life. In practical terms, of course, she would become the love of his life, his wife of more than half-a-century and the perfect partner in his career. But symbolically, the meeting seemed to change his luck. For twenty-two years, his life—although filled with promise—had been defined chiefly by poverty and tragedy. Now, suddenly, things began to go right. Within a year after that night in June, all the forces that would shape his future were in place, and it wouldn't be long after that before Al would take control of those forces to build a musical dynasty and a living monument.

Lena Baer operated the Lafayette Conservatory of Music at the corner of Seventh and Columbia streets, and in the summer of 1930, her business was surprisingly good. So good, in fact, that she needed another voice teacher. When she heard that Al Stewart was back in town, she saw a chance to help out a young man and to improve her little school at the same time. Although he had completed only a year of study at DePauw, Al's musical education was better than that of most of her instructors. Besides his piano study, he had had five years of private voice lessons as a youth. There was no question about his ability, and besides, he was well enough known that he might bring in more students. Al immediately accepted the invitation to teach at the conservatory, and Miss Baer gave him the front studio with its big concert grand.

Although the economic hard times had robbed many families of such luxuries as music lessons, there was no shortage of students. Thirty-five to forty of them each week came to study voice with Al. Most of these were local children, but a handful of Purdue students came as well. Al couldn't believe his good fortune: "The exciting thing was that I was doing the thing I most wanted to do—and getting paid for it. I was getting experience in the field I dearly loved, and I found that I did understand voice." It was at Miss Baer's studio that Al began to develop the teaching techniques that would be among the most successful in American choral music. Fundamental to this was his insistence that singers not be intimidated by music:

> It just isn't that difficult to learn to sing. Music is sound delivered at controlled pace and pitch, and that's all there is to it. When singers learn how to follow a good director, you can have good results. They don't have to be able to read music. Darn few people can read music chorally. They just read by position. The only man I've ever known who could *really* read music was Bill Luhman. He could look at something he'd never seen or heard before and just give it to you in key—no pitch thrown at him from the piano or anything. But that was a special gift. Most of us have to have a little help. There's no reason to let the music scare you.
>
> Everybody's better off if they just relax and try to have fun. I get a kick out of listening to the warm-up exercises some groups go through—all this mee-mee-mee-mee-mee-meee stuff. I just have them sing "How Dry I Am" or something easy. That gets the throat clear and the breath working, and it gets people in the mood to sing, too. It's easy for some people to forget that we're supposed to have a good time.

Just before Purdue classes started in September 1930, Carolyn Shoemaker, dean of women at the university, called Al on the telephone and said, "I wonder if we could talk to you about your coming in to direct our Women's Glee Club?"

Al didn't think the offer was very promising. For one thing, the compensation, a percentage of ticket-sale proceeds, was nominal at best—even by depression standards. For another, the Women's Glee Club, like other Purdue singing groups of the era, was bereft of money, reputation and prospects. An annual concert in tiny Fowler Hall drew sparse crowds. Otherwise the club, sponsored by the Mortar Board Society, existed primarily for the amusement of its own members. But Al demurred for other reasons.

"I don't think that would work out very well," he told the dean. "Those girls are too near my own age. I'd have too much difficulty with them."

But Carolyn Shoemaker and Mortar Board President Alma Williams (later Hawkins) were determined to get a director who knew music for their girls.

"I'll make a deal with you," the dean said. "You handle the music, and I'll handle the discipline."

And that's what they did. Al began going twice a week to rehearse the women on campus. Dean Shoemaker came to each rehearsal and listened quietly to make sure there was no nonsense. This arrangement lasted for about a month. Then, after an hour of listening to the new director threaten, cajole and occasionally bully the altos and sopranos, she called Al aside and said: "I'm going back to my office. You don't need me here. You're a lot tougher on these girls than I'd ever be. Just keep it up."

And so the directing style that would mold motley collections of farm boys and city kids into polished vocal ensembles got its first official endorsement. In 1930, Al didn't really know how one went about directing a college glee club, but as he would for more than forty years, he did what his instincts told him to do. The years of musical training—both the study and the performance—combined with his natural feel for human nature, and he got results. Perhaps those early years of watching his father put the fear of God into a congregation had left a mark. Certainly he had learned from Robert McCutcheon at DePauw, but the final product—what came out in rehearsal and onstage—was 100 percent Al Stewart. He could demand, he could plead, he could cheerlead, he could praise and he could damn well throw you out if you didn't pay attention. The trick was in knowing exactly when and for how long to do each, and Al always seemed to know. One of his guiding precepts became, "There are no rules until you break one."

The result was a fast transformation of the Women's Glee Club from cheerful mediocrity to zesty competence. If he hadn't known it before, Al found out then that young people can thrive under assertive leadership. They worked harder, they accepted his criticism, and they had a better time than they did singing on their own. Music was fun in Al's lexicon. When you combined it with hard work, it was still fun, and it was better music.

By the end of a semester, the Purdue Women's Glee Club was sounding pretty good to Al. They sang the traditional music and religious numbers that were the backbone of women's choral singing. But musically, Al found the group limiting. It was fine as far as it went, and he wanted to hold the ground he'd gained with the women, but his real preference had always been, and always would be, for mixed-voice choirs. There had to be other women on campus who could sing, and there certainly were plenty of men. To Al, a university choir was a natural way to fill a musical vacuum at Purdue. Thinking that his success with the Women's Glee Club would give him some leverage, he conceived the idea of getting the university to fund a choir, including a small salary for its director—Al Stewart.

Armed with his idea and his natural store of confidence, Al set out one January day to make his proposal to Edward C. Elliott, the president of Purdue. The twenty-three years (1922–45) in which Edward Charles Elliott sat in the presidential office were arguably the most important in Purdue's history. He took over a little state college with no real reputation outside Indiana and made it a great learning center. Purdue reached national stature academically and athletically under his leadership, and it doubled its enrollment, from a little over 3,000 students to more than 7,000. This growth was accompanied by a dozen major building additions, which included what are now Ross-Ade Stadium, the Hovde Hall of Administration, the Physics Building and the Electrical Engineering Building. The value of the physical plant more than tripled in an age when there was no such thing as an annual inflation rate. By the time Elliott retired in 1945, Purdue was ready for the enormous enrollment increases the post-World War II era would bring, and for the research boom that also was an aftermath of the war. Although research had expanded and improved under Elliott, it was the university's teaching element that took precedence. He had begun his career teaching high school in Leadville, Colorado, and although he quickly was promoted and spent most of his career as an administrator, he always thought of himself as a schoolteacher.

Elliott was chancellor of the University of Montana in 1921 when Winthrop Stone, president of Purdue, fell to his death while climbing Mount Eon in the Canadian Rockies. Born in Chicago in 1874, Elliott grew up in North Platte, Iowa, still a frontier town in those days. As a boy, Elliott once dried himself and his clothes before the fire of Buffalo Bill Cody after falling through the ice of a local pond. Elliott ran Purdue with as much authority as any university president ever has had, and the relatively small size of the institution in those days allowed him to know the place intimately. Nothing happened at Purdue unless Edward Elliott said it would happen.

Although he was barely five feet ten inches tall in his shoes, people thought of Elliott as a tall man. He was ascetically thin with deep-set eyes, a nose large enough to look down, and a massive authoritarian chin. An excellent public speaker, as well as a good conversationalist, Elliott spoke in slow, deep, rolling tones and was fond of alliteration. At ceremonies celebrating his first ten years at Purdue he said, "they have been years filled with adventures—adventures in dreaming and doing; in success and in failure; in prosperity and poverty; in drudgery and in delight; in responsibility and in helplessness; adventures with foes and with friends."

Al Stewart was neither friend nor foe as he made his way across campus to Elliott's office in the rear of Eliza Fowler Hall. He had never met the president, and he didn't know where he stood. As it turned out, he would not know for several years where he stood with Elliott, but he found out quickly who would be making the decisions.

One of the things Elliott liked about running a university in Indiana was the clear mission statement under which each of the two major institutions worked. Purdue taught engineering, agriculture, pharmacy, some science and whatever support courses were necessary. Indiana University took care of the liberal arts, medicine, and—among other things—music. This arrangement appealed to Elliott because it allowed the two institutions to complement each other. He had found the spirit of cooperation in Indiana a refreshing change from Montana, where the universities operated in an environment of what he considered destructive competition.

Now here was this brash young nobody—too handsome for his own good, hair combed like the dandies of the day, smile too broad to be sincere—asking for money to start a musical group. Elliott sat behind his big wooden desk and listened as Al's eager spiel ran down. Then he stood up and struck the top of the desk with the flat of his hand. "Never!" he shouted. "Never, as long as I am president, will this university spend one damn penny for music on this campus, young man. Get that through your head!"

An early experiment with choreography was this stylized performance by the 1933–34 Women's Glee Club Revue.

The numbers in the Women's Glee Club were growing in 1936, when this picture was taken.

Al was not prepared with a fall-back position, and he was, by his own description, "scared to death" of the president, but he wanted to salvage something from the meeting. He wasn't about to argue with Elliott's refusal, but he finally found the courage to say, "All right, sir, but do you mind if I just use the name Purdue University Choir? Would you object to that if I don't ask for any money?"

Elliott moved out from behind the desk and walked over to the window. He looked out and rubbed his chin. Finally, he turned around and said, "No, I don't see any harm in that. Not if you're damn fool enough. But you know, I think you *are* a damn fool, and I think you'll probably do it."

When he began to understand the president's management style, Al realized that the intimidation and the challenge were Elliott's way of getting things done and of weeding out people with big ideas but half-hearted commitments. At the time, though, Al thought he probably was as big a fool as the president had called him. He had barely enough money to live on, and now he had to start a choir with no financial support.

But start the choir he did. It was a small group patterned after the one in which he had sung at DePauw under Robert McCutcheon. Before the semester was over, the Purdue University Choir had developed a campus reputation. Even President Elliott began to have the student group booked onto special programs for trustees, visiting dignitaries and alumni groups. Trying to bring the choir's appearance up to the level of its performance, Al one day went into Southworth's Bookstore and bought a set of academic robes, which he thought would serve as choir robes. He charged them to the Purdue University Choir, with no idea of when or how he would be able to pay for them. "I just felt we had to have something that made us look like a real choir," he said. "Image is just so important in a performance, and if you look like a raggedy-ass outfit, that's what people will think you sound like. I wasn't going to cheat the store out of the cost of those robes, but I sure didn't know where I would get the money either. I just hoped something would happen."

Elliott noticed the robes the next time the choir performed, and commented on them. Not long after that, he asked Al if he needed anything for the choir. "I'd like to get their robes paid for," Al answered quickly.

"How much?" Elliot asked. Al told him.

"That's too damn much!" the president retorted, and he walked away.

The choir kept on singing, and Al kept putting off the first payment until one Saturday night about three weeks later when the president approached Al after another concert.

"Young man," he growled, "unless the wind blows me off the face of the earth, come Monday morning, I'll pay for those damn robes." Thus did Elliott—for the only time in their association—break a promise to Al Stewart. In the process, he took the first step toward becoming the godfather of music at Purdue. Through the years, he must have reflected on the irony of his situation, but once he had made a decision to support musical groups, he never wavered. Two things happened to bring about the complete reversal of his attitude: First of all, Al Stewart won his respect. From the first meeting when Elliott's intimidation had failed to break down Al's determination to establish a choir, through a series of similar confrontations, Elliott, with whom everyone agreed all the time, learned that his music director had priorities other than pleasing the president. Al knew what he wanted, and he would protect his own interests, and if he disagreed with the president, he said so. Elliott found that kind of honesty rare, and he respected it. The second thing was Elliott's recognition of the public-relations benefits that the music was bringing to Purdue. The president knew a bargain when he saw it. As a result, music at Purdue eventually began to receive not only pretty much everything Al asked for, but a good bit more. Elliott was a generous godfather.

Chapter 6

The Women's Glee Club, 1931–32. Manager Wilma Clark is seated in the middle of the front row. Carolyn Shoemaker, then dean of women at Purdue, asked Al to direct the group in 1930.

THE MUSIC PENTHOUSE

With the Women's Glee Club well established and the University Choir in ever-increasing demand for campus entertainment, it was obvious to everyone concerned with music that Al Stewart could make things happen. The Men's Glee Club had continued as a separate enterprise. Its checkered history had been marred by inconsistency, perhaps because of the club's practice of allowing the elected student managers to hire and fire the director. This produced not only some fast turnovers on the podium, but an organization that lacked strength at the top.

Organized choral music at Purdue goes back to 1891 when a Chapel Choir was founded. Written records on the short-lived group are few, but the university yearbook, *Debris*, carried this epitaph in 1892:

> Born Monday, September 9, 1891 at Purdue University—the Chapel Choir. Departed this life—Tuesday, April 6, 1892. Age: 6 months—26 days.

In 1893, eleven of the university's 638 students founded the original Men's Glee Club. Professor Cyrus Dadswell, organist at St. John's Church in Lafayette, was the director; Larry Downs was the manager, and G. W. Remington was the secretary.

We don't know about the quality of music that early Glee Club sang, but records show that it was an organization with leadership problems. It had five different directors in its first five years of existence, and the turnover rate never slowed down very much. In 1910, a student, E. J. Wotawa, directed the singers. Wotawa later composed the music to the fight song, "Hail Purdue," which he dedicated to the Glee Club.

Paul T. Smith took over as director in 1920 and brought a measure of stability to the organization until his sudden death in 1927. The podium was occupied by Professors J. T. Gunn and Edward Frank briefly before Smith's widow became the director.

Helen Smith was still director in 1932 when Al got his first concession from President Elliott. No doubt prompted by the sudden success of the University Choir and the Women's Glee Club, several Men's Glee Club members visited Al one day and asked if he would be interested in directing their group. If Al was tempted to take the job, he didn't let on to the boys: "I emphatically said, 'No, I would not.' I told them Mrs. Smith was doing a fine job, and they had no reason to change. I wasn't about to let them use me as an excuse to fire Mrs. Smith. That was the end of it. The boys thanked me and left."

But at the end of the school year, Mrs. Smith decided on her own to resign from the Glee Club. The contingent came back to Al and asked again. This time he accepted, but he insisted on a change that he always would regard as the smartest move he ever made as director of the Glee Club. "The first thing I did was to eliminate the possibility of being fired," he said. "I demanded that they change their rules so that the officers of the club were appointed by me, rather than elected. After that, they were working for me, instead of my working for them. They sure as hell would have fired me if they could have—lots of times—if I hadn't done that."

The new system wasn't democratic, but it was functional, and it gave the organization a continuity that few musical groups achieve. Under forty-two years of Al Stewart and the subsequent leadership of Bill Luhman and Bill Allen, the Glee Club evolved musically and was influenced by popular trends from blues to new wave, but it kept its identity.

Purdue now had a Men's Glee Club, a Women's Glee Club, and a University Choir, all under the directorship of Al Stewart, whom Purdue was not paying for his efforts. He was still teaching voice at the Lafayette Conservatory of Music, helping out at the Luna Theater, and sleeping on a cot in his mother's dining room to allow her to rent out his bedroom.

President Elliott was determined to treat music as an auxiliary enterprise of the university, so the groups were expected to pay their own way, just as the athletic teams did. Since choral singing could not fill a stadium the way a football game could, and since there was no tradition of quality to help sell tickets to concerts, Al's Purdue Musical Organizations, as he started to call them, couldn't bring in much money. Some early funding came from Indianapolis pharmaceutical magnate Joshua K. Lilly, who liked the idea of encouraging music on campus. He sent Elliott regular checks to support the groups.

Still, the organizations were campus orphans. For one thing, they had no regular place to rehearse. As quickly as Al would find an empty room in the Purdue Memorial Union or an unoccupied classroom, another activity with more importance or clout would come along, and the singers would be muscled out. The Purdue Musical Organizations had no phone number on campus, and if they had an office, it was in Al's hip pocket.

The plight of the musical organizations eventually was noticed by Lillian Stewart, the wife of R. B. Stewart, then comptroller of the university. The Stewarts, who were no relation to Al, were colossal figures on campus. R. B. was a monetary wizard, who single-handedly invented many aspects of modern university financing, and Lillian was an irrepressible "doer." She loved to get involved with worthwhile projects, and more often than not, she ended up running them. She liked the singing of Al Stewart's student groups, and when she heard about their lack of rehearsal space, she had an easy solution.

"Why don't you come over to our house and rehearse?" she asked. "We have a piano, and I'd love to listen." The Stewarts lived at the corner of Fifth and University streets—virtually on the campus—so a few nights later, Al assembled the University Choir in R. B. and Lillian Stewart's living room. They were no more boisterous than twenty or so college students usually are, and the group got in two hours of hard practice. As he was packing up his music before leaving, Al thanked his hostess and asked, "Isn't Mr. Stewart coming home tonight? I haven't seen him."

"Oh, he's here," Mrs. Stewart said sweetly. "He's upstairs with a sick headache."

The next morning, Al was in R. B. Stewart's University Hall office, having been summoned by Miss Suppart, R. B.'s formidable secretary. R. B. got right to the point. "Young man," he said, "you can't do things like this to people. They have a right to peace and quiet in their own homes. When you leave

The Purdue Concert Choir of 1931 was one of the first of Al Stewart's groups to entertain off campus and the one he credited with establishing his reputation.

One of the very first Purdue musical groups—the Glee Club of 1894.

This ensemble photographed in 1926 displayed an unusual wardrobe blend. Early Glee Club organizations frequently were associated with mandolin clubs, which were popular at Purdue in the early twentieth century.

here, I want you to hunt this campus until you find a place where you think you can hold your rehearsals. Then come back and tell me what you've found and we'll see what we can do."

Al spent several days, starting in basements and working his way up to attics. There are an immense number of rooms on any university campus, but very few superfluous ones, and every office or classroom or closet seemed to have some indispensable purpose. One room, being used for storage in the old Electrical Engineering Building, looked promising, but its owners refused to give it up.

The place he finally found was not exactly under R. B. Stewart's nose, but it was right over his head. A steep flight of steps led up to a room on the top floor of University Hall. The founding meeting of the Big Ten Conference had been held there in 1895, but when Al stuck his head in the door for the first time, the room was being used for the building of scenery for the university's playshop. Scenery flats were laid on the floor to be painted, brushes were cleaned by wiping them on the walls, and a paint-spattered old piano was used as a makeshift sawhorse.

R. B. told the theater group that its operation was a fire hazard in an old building like University Hall. He gave them forty-eight hours to move the scenery to the sub-basement of the union. Then he told Al that the rehearsal hall was all his. He could do anything he wanted with the room, R. B. said, as long as he didn't spend any money. So Al and his students climbed up to the Music Penthouse, as they immediately began calling it. They inched along the floor with silver knives, trying to scrape up the dried paint and putty. They swept and dusted and scrubbed, but the room still looked like a scenery-painting room when Lillian Stewart came to visit. She was appalled.

"This is filthy!" she said. "It's got to be painted."

Al said he had strict orders from Mrs. Stewart's husband not to spend any money on the area. Lillian exited muttering something that sounded like, "We'll see about that."

The next day, as he climbed the stairs to the fourth floor, Al smelled paint. When he got to the Music Penthouse, he found a crew of university physical-plant workers painting the room.

For the first time, music had a home at Purdue, and humble as it was, there was no place like it as far as Al and his singers were concerned. They borrowed a mismatched assortment of chairs from various offices. For a desk, Al found an old library table. They lovingly draped red oilcloth across the tops of the high old windows. With a run of about twenty feet, the more athletic of the students could leap up into the window wells to raise and lower the windows. They got the "sawhorse" tuned well enough to play accompaniment. Al would never settle for anything so pathetic again, but in 1932, it was beautiful. "We did all right there," he said. "Maybe it was just an attic, but it was a palace as far as I was concerned. It was the first time I felt like we really belonged on campus."

But the future of the Purdue Musical Organizations was far from secure. They owed their existence and the modest progress they had made primarily to the fact that their director didn't have a real job. While it was true that music was what Al loved most, and he was enjoying the challenge of scraping out an existence for the groups against what seemed to be administrative indifference, he wouldn't have had the luxury of passing up an opportunity for full-time employment. He and the rest of his family needed the money too badly. Had such an offer come along, the fragile structure he had put together might not have survived.

Al did earn some money from his Purdue involvement in those early days. His arrangement called for him to get 50 percent of the proceeds from concert ticket sales. He collected at the end of the academic year, and his share in the spring of 1932 was a little over $200.

When the students returned that fall, Al decided it was time to try to take his groups off campus. Until then, the student singers entertained only locally. There was no money for travel, and there had never been a demand for the university's singers. Al thought that if he could start booking "real" jobs, he and the organizations might make a little more money. He also reasoned that a good start as the 1932 school year began might bring more business throughout the year.

Al brainstormed this concept with the student manager he had selected, Theo "Pinky" Agnew. Characteristically, Al wanted to start big, and the two of them came up with the idea of trying to book a choir into the Circle Theater, the most prestigious showplace in Indianapolis. They thought they might have a chance to put on a show over the Thanksgiving weekend. Neither Al nor Pinky had a car—or access to a car—so one September morning, dressed in their best suits, they started hitchhiking down U. S. 52 to meet with the manager of the Circle and try to convince him to hire the Purdue Concert Choir. At that time, the "Concert Choir" existed only in their minds, but Al was confident he could organize and properly rehearse such a group if he could get a booking.

The manager of the theater listened politely as the two earnest young men from Purdue extolled the virtues of their choir and the successes of the growing music program at their university. He did have an opening during the Thanksgiving weekend, and he would be willing to book the choir on a percentage basis. Al and Pinky could hardly believe their success. They had done their best to impress the manager with their prosperity, so that he wouldn't think they really *needed* the booking. As they got up to leave, he said, "Where's your car?"

Al thought fast. "It's over at the Circle Motor Inn," he said. That was a parking garage just off the circle.

"Good," the manager replied. "I can walk over with you. I have to stop by the Indiana Theater."

When they got to the garage, Al put out his hand and said, "It's been very nice talking with you. Thanks. We'll see you in November." He was praying the man wouldn't follow him into the garage. Pinky shook hands, too, and the manager, to their relief, walked on. They went into the garage and waited until he was safely out of sight before they started thumbing a ride back to Lafayette.

"As far as we were concerned, we'd just landed the biggest job anybody ever had," Al said. "We four-flushed our way through that deal to put on our first concert, but we delivered. We put on a good show for them, and we made a little money, too. It took a lot of nerve to do that, but nerve was about all we had."

Chapter 7

The human Christmas tree has been a mainstay of Christmas Shows through the years. This one was formed by female P.M.O. members in 1953.

HOLIDAY MAGIC

Throughout the 1932–33 school year, things went well for the singing groups. At a campus where student musical efforts usually had been haphazard at best, the consistent quality of Al Stewart's organizations was a pleasant surprise. President Elliott continued to use the University Choir to entertain guests, and Al was able to book several more off-campus concerts after the Thanksgiving success in Indianapolis. By the spring of 1933, Al began to hear from other colleges that wanted to start or build up singing programs. Compelling words, like "salary" and "contract," were spoken as they asked if he'd ever thought of leaving Purdue.

He didn't want to leave, of course, but he had to get on with the business of making a living. He and Charlotte were eager to get married, and he felt obligated to help support his younger brothers. While he tried to decide what to do, he told his students that they probably would have to find a new director in the fall. They went straight to President Elliott. In June of 1933, Al was summoned to the president's office.

"Several students have been to see me," Elliott said. "They tell me you've had some offers to go elsewhere."

"That's right," Al answered.

"Are you thinking of accepting one of them?"

"Yes sir, I am."

Elliott looked disappointed. "But you've been doing very well here," he said. "Suppose I give you $100 a month, starting in September. Would you consider staying on?"

To Al, the words were a miracle. At that point in his life, he could imagine nothing better than to get paid a living wage for what he had been doing almost for free at Purdue. He and Charlotte could get married, and they wouldn't have to start over in a strange town. But Al didn't say any of this to the president. Instead, he blurted: "This means I won't have to sleep in the dining room any more."

Elliott didn't understand the joke. "I don't know anything about your dining room, young man," he growled. "You sleep anywhere you please."

Al floated out the door and across campus to the apartment of Murray and Virginia McKee, where he was meeting Charlotte for dinner that night. They immediately started making wedding plans. Because neither of their families could afford a wedding, they decided on a "depression elopement." They would elope, but they would tell their parents first. After making arrangements to rent a tiny four-room house at the corner of Fourth and Russell streets, they set the date for June 25, 1933, a Sunday. Before leaving that morning, they had to attend services at the Central Presbyterian Church. Al had just gotten a job as choir director, and he had scheduled his first rehearsal for that day.

As soon as they left the church, they started for Indianapolis in Al's battered old Ford Coupe. It rained most of the trip, and they used their bathing suits to mop up the water that was pouring in through the roof. By the time they got to Indianapolis, the sun had come out, and they spent the afternoon riding the rides at Riverside Amusement Park. Early that evening, they slipped down to Jamestown, Indiana, where Albert Miller now was a pastor. He married Al and Charlotte in his living room, with the McKees as witnesses.

That night, Al and Charlotte drove back to their little house in West Lafayette—the first of twelve homes they would occupy during their fifty-one years of marriage. The next morning, they went over to the Friends' house, where Al's mother and brothers met them for a day of celebration.

The Stewarts spent the summer making plans for the things they could do now that music was officially accepted at Purdue. Being on the payroll freed Al to spend time selecting music, doing arrangements, scheduling more off-campus concerts. All of these things would refine his product and allow him to prove more emphatically that music was worth the money Elliott was spending on it. Al didn't know it yet, but the president already had decided that the Purdue Musical Organizations were a blue-chip investment. The positive impact the singers had on visitors, the public relations value of clean-cut Purdue students singing all over the state, the little extra something that the choir and glee clubs added to campus events were all positive factors, and these hadn't been lost on the shrewd Elliott. He was getting a bargain and he knew it. Furthermore, he had decided he liked the determined young director.

In September, Elliott and his wife, Elizabeth, invited Al and Charlotte to their home on Seventh Street in Lafayette for dinner with the Purdue Board of Trustees. The newlyweds were honored, but just intimidated enough to do the wrong thing. The invitation was for dinner at seven, but they wanted to avoid the awkwardness of having to make conversation beforehand. Besides, neither of them drank alcohol at the time, and they weren't sure it was proper to turn down a pre-dinner drink. They decided they would be safest to arrive just a few minutes after seven. "Pace," the Elliotts' very proper butler, opened the door for Al's ring at six minutes after the hour. Right behind the servant was the president, carrying his napkin and chewing his food.

"Come in," Elliott said. "We never embarrass our guests by making them think they're important enough to wait for."

Al and Charlotte slunk into the dining room. Al was seated on Mrs. Elliott's right, while Charlotte was asked to join some of the trustees in the sunroom. Throughout the dinner, Al couldn't keep his feet still because of his nervousness. He barely tasted his food, but he did notice that the waiters kept coming into the dining room and then leaving with no apparent purpose. Finally, Mrs. Elliott leaned over and whispered, "Dear boy, I believe you have your foot on the service bell."

Ultimately, the evening was saved when Charlotte was asked to sing. On that familiar ground, the young couple could relax and enjoy the fact that the president of the university thought they were worthy of eating dinner with the Purdue trustees.

Suddenly, it seemed that Al could do nothing wrong. He had Elliott's blessing, and even his friendship. Where there had been only the most tentative and disorganized music programs at Purdue before, now there were dynamic, growing organizations, all under Al Stewart. They sang better than anyone had sung before at Purdue. They brought in some money; they impressed people all over the state. Besides the glee clubs and the various choirs, Al organized a small orchestra to provide accompaniment and dinner and dance music.

The Men's Glee Club had come under Al's direction comparatively late, but it wasn't long before he noticed that this group produced the most powerful reaction in audiences. Al was first and last an entertainer, and he wasn't going to fight his audiences. "There is something about a male group that people react to," he said. "It's powerful, and it's sexy. You can produce emotional highs and lows that you can't get with anything else."

Very soon, the Men's Glee Club was the headliner. Al channeled his best male voices into it, and he spent more time on the programming. With the traditional and religious music the Glee Club had always sung, he began to mix popular music and novelty songs and found that he could, in the time it took to put on a concert, take an audience through every human emotion. "There aren't too many things I can do really well," he would say, "but being an audience is one of them. I can walk into a room and *know* what will work with *those* people on *that* night. I don't know how I know it, but I do, and I've never doubted my ability to do that. That's why I never published a program ahead of time, because I might walk in and find that a certain number or the whole program was wrong, and I would be stuck with it."

Decades later people would marvel at the musical empire Al Stewart had built at a university that had no music school and still paid very little to support his programs. He would always insist that he never planned any growth or expansion—that he tried new ideas because they were interesting, keeping only the things that worked. Time after time, preparation met opportunity, and Al's good fortune kept rolling along, but it would get even better.

On a spring day in 1937, Elliott summoned Al to the presidential office in Fowler Hall and, without wasting any words, dropped a bombshell.

"Tomorrow, my new executive building will be finished, and I'm going to move in," he said. "You're the only person at the university who hasn't asked me for this building, and that's why I'm going to give it to you." Elliott swept his gaze around the office. "I'm taking my books and my files. Everything else will be left just as it is," he said. "This will be your office. I'm leaving at ten in the morning. You can come in then." Al couldn't believe what he was hearing. He had considered himself lucky to have the fourth-floor garret in University Hall, and now he had been given a beautiful stone building with a huge office and plenty of space for his singers. But Elliott was not through yet.

The next morning, promptly at ten, Al walked into the president's office. Elliott rose from his desk—the same one he had once pounded so formidably—and said, "It's all yours, son." He started to walk out, but paused and returned. "Of course," he said, "you'll have enough sense to make a rehearsal room out of the trustees' room upstairs." He started for the door again, but returned once more, looking thoughtful. "By the way," he added, "better get yourself a secretary. You can't run a building like this one without a secretary—I'll pay for it. Oh, and you better get an assistant, too. It looks like you're going to get more and more to do around this place. You're just like the camel that got his head in the tent and wouldn't quit until he had torn the tent down.

"Now remember," the president continued, "the assistant isn't so you can do twice as much—it's so you can do half as much; you work too hard. Send the assistant on jobs, and stay home once in a while—unless it's *my* job. Then I expect to see you there."

Elliott walked out, and Al sat contemplating what had just happened to him. Music suddenly was in the big time at Purdue. He had a staff and a building with everything he needed. Fowler Hall was equipped with office space and a 500-seat performing hall. There were pianos in his office, in the rehearsal room and onstage. Most important of all, he had a clear mandate from the president to keep building. Of all the departments at Purdue that could have benefited by acquiring Fowler Hall, Elliott had chosen the musical organizations. Was it possible that Al had more status than the deans and department heads who had vied for the building? Elliott never explained his motives, but he was the kind of president who could see beyond the considerations of internal politics. He knew that the growing excellence of Al's programs was helping Purdue in ways that could never be documented or quantified. Thousands of people throughout the state and even beyond, to Chicago, Louisville and other major cities, now were hearing Purdue students sing. This might not make them sit down and write checks to the university or decide on the spot to send their children to Purdue, but it left them with a clear and pleasant memory associated with the university's name. Furthermore, the musical organizations had an obvious positive effect on campus morale—not only on the students who sang, but on everyone who felt pride in the quality of the programs Al staged.

The president also probably understood the special delight Purdue people took in bragging that the glee clubs and the choirs—good as they were—were the products of a university that had no music school and didn't really fund the musical organizations. Although Elliott now was paying salaries for Al and his small staff and was maintaining a building for them, the groups continued to finance their own trips and other expenses.

It was typical of Elliott's management style that he handed Al the tools and the staff to make the music program far bigger and better than had seemed possible, but had given no clear instructions for growth and change. He knew the sort of man he had in Al Stewart, and he was sure that, left alone, the director would move ahead—probably in ways Elliott couldn't predict—but the president was willing to allow Al free rein, at least for as long as good things kept happening.

Al believed the president had decided to support him on March 2, 1933. That was the day Dean Carolyn Shoemaker died unexpectedly. The dean had been Al's benefactress at Purdue, and her sudden death was a powerful personal blow for Al. "Dr. Elliott sensed my concern," he said. "And I know it was then that he decided to support me all the way. From that day until the day he died, he never turned down a request I made."

As his first assistant director, Al hired Joseph M. Ragains. Ragains had been teaching music in a public school in Tipton County, Indiana. His brother, Robert, who sang in Al's choir at Central Presbyterian, recommended him for the job. Edith Mills, who had been Charlotte's roommate in the Alpha Phi sorority house at DePauw, became Al's first secretary. She had acquired good clerical skills but she also was a fine pianist, who had majored in music at DePauw. So Al had a built-in back-up accompanist, as well as a secretary who wouldn't be confused by musical terminology. Ragains was a good organizer

What would Christmas be without kids? The annual holiday extravaganza always incorporates a large number of youngsters. This group was featured on the Elliott Hall of Music stage in 1974.

Larry Hausenfluck was "The Stingiest Man in Town" in 1960. The musical version of Dickens's *A Christmas Carol* is a regular part of Christmas Shows.

P.M.O.'s Choral Club provided the music, while a "living doll" added a holiday touch in this scene from the 1980 Christmas Show.

High-kicking Choral Club members formed a Christmas chorus line in 1981, while other members of the women's group harmonized with the Glee Club.

The year was 1982, the season Christmas; the group was the University Choir. Whatever the song was, the singers were intent on following Bill Allen's direction and Dennis Yount's accompaniment.

The Purdue Belles of 1980. Both bell groups have become favorites on Christmas Show programs.

Another version of the living Christmas tree, as staged in 1982. The sets have grown more elaborate through the years, but the spirit has stayed the same.

and a competent director, who could fill in for Al, help run the organization, and direct the orchestra.

The acquisition of Fowler Hall was a great leap forward for the musical organizations, but actually Al had begun to stage ambitious entertainments in its auditorium four years earlier. He had toyed with the idea of some kind of Christmas show for some time before taking action in 1933. As soon as the students returned in the fall he started rehearsing them, designing sets and costumes and putting together a program that would feature traditional and religious music. "It was a good show," Al would reflect later. "I put everything I had into it, and the kids really worked hard. But it was one of the biggest disappointments of my life."

Admission was free to the Fowler Hall extravaganza, which featured all the student singing groups, but despite the best promotion campaign Al could muster, a small crowd of about 200 people showed up. Al was crushed. For once, he doubted his ability to gauge popular choice. This had started out as the greatest year of his life, and he had ended it by overestimating the drawing power of his singers. He confided this disappointment to R. T. Friend, who tried to console his son-in-law. Was the show any good? R. T. asked. Al said it was damn good. Was he sure? Of course he was sure! Then keep doing it until people start coming, the older man urged.

Al took R. T.'s advice, because it agreed with his own instinct. He knew that the few who had come to that first show were impressed. Perhaps they would spread the word. Sure enough, the attendance increased the following year, and it kept going up, as people returned year after year, meanwhile telling their friends and relatives about the great free show at Purdue. Soon the appeal outgrew Fowler Hall, but with the completion of the vast Hall of Music in 1940, the pressure was eased temporarily. By 1947, though, even more than 6,000 seats in the Hall of Music couldn't come close to handling the demand, so a second performance was added. In 1954, the Christmas Show went to a third performance, and, at the direction of President Frederick Hovde, admission was charged—one dollar for adults, fifty cents for children and college students. The fee helped pay for the show's rising production costs, but it also was intended to hold down the size of the crowds.

It didn't work. The crowds kept coming, despite subsequent price increases and the addition of still more shows. Until 1962, seating remained on a first-come-first-served basis. That year, two things happened which forced the institution of a reserved seating policy. In the rush for choice seats at the front of the auditorium, an elderly woman was knocked down and nearly trampled. The victim, ironically, was Ethel Stewart—Al's mother; she wasn't hurt seriously. That same year, two busloads of people from Michigan were turned away after a trip to West Lafayette in a snowstorm. Al and Hovde recognized that a public relations bonanza was being turned into a potential disaster. The Purdue Musical Organizations had a "festival seating" crisis over Christmas carols long before rock music concerts faced the same kind of problems.

In 1964, a fourth show was added, and all seats for the Christmas Show were reserved. In 1967, a fifth show was added, and the next year a sixth—with dead sellouts for every performance. The number of shows was cut back to five in 1972 in deference to the entertainers' study schedules. Ever since then, more than 30,000 people have watched the P.M.O. Christmas Show every year, and an unknown number have been disappointed by failure to get tickets. Although the show is a money-maker for P.M.O., helping to fund scholarships for members and to pay for travel and other expenses, ticket prices traditionally have been kept low in the spirit of offering the performance as a Christmas treat.

Would Al Stewart have given up the whole idea if his father-in-law hadn't encouraged him after that initial disappointment? Probably not. Al knew he had a good production, and he believed in his gift for judging what appealed. The secret of the Christmas Show, he said, was the season itself. "You can do anything at Christmastime. People want to be entertained in an upbeat way. You can get away with being sentimental and even corny, because that's the way people want to feel once a year." Of course, he had to combine the easy spirit of the season with good-quality shows, and it helped that the holiday feeling matched up nicely with the rich traditional approach the P.M.O. groups used year-round. In terms of audience appeal and financial payback, the Purdue Christmas extravaganza may be the most successful annual amateur production in the country.

The business of putting the show together is a Herculean feat. In a matter of about two months, six musical groups, including several hundred students, are drawn into a single production. Since the groups seldom perform together the rest of the year, and since there is about a 25 percent annual turnover of the members, rough spots abound in the initial rehearsals. The enormous logistics of the production are aggravated by the fact that the show comes together at about the same time Purdue students are heading into final exams for the semester. But one of the secrets Al and his successors learned early was that young people, when they work in a well-disciplined environment, are capable of remarkable feats—far more than they realize themselves. Even those in difficult academic disciplines often get excellent grades while devoting time to extracurricular activities. In fact, P.M.O. members consistently are above university averages in their grade indexes, and their success may be because of—rather than in spite of—the extra time they put into their singing.

For Al Stewart, the Christmas convocations produced forty years of happy memories and two minutes of sheer terror. The latter occurred at the beginning of the first performance during one of the World War II years. The show opened with the lights down in the Hall of Music and a long line of students carrying candles in solemn dignity across the rear of the darkened stage. A girl in the line noticed self-consciously that her new high heels were producing a loud tapping sound with each step. Afraid that the noise would destroy the effect of the opening in the otherwise-silent hall, she was glad to see that she would pass right next to what looked like a rubber floor mat on the stage. She inched to her right so that she could walk across the mat—and stepped straight into an open trap door. Waiting upstage, Al saw only the swift descent and disappearance of the candle, but he knew immediately what had happened. "I lived three lifetimes before I got down that pit," he said. "By the time I got there, a soldier and a Marine were there. One of them had covered her up, and the other had rolled his coat up under her head. She had fallen ten or twelve feet. I said, 'Are you hurt?' and she said, 'You know, I'm really not. I must have been so relaxed when I fell that it just didn't hurt me.'" A few minutes later, Al was able to tell the audience: "Please don't worry about the young lady who fell earlier. She's up here in the choir right now."

Chapter 8

Edward C. Elliott proved to be a generous godfather to the young Purdue Musical Organizations. He secured $1.2 million in federal and state funds to build a hall of music at Purdue. This photo shows the building's elegant front lobby.

MILLION-DOLLAR PLAYHOUSE

In the spring of 1938, President Elliott sent for Al and offered him a new opportunity. "I want you to get some more formal music education," Elliott told him. "Pick out the place you'd like to go, and I'll help you." Al decided on the American Conservatory of Music in Chicago. Charlotte, who still was soloing extensively with the Glee Club, decided to take the opportunity to study at the same time. Their first daughter, Sonya, had been born in 1937, so they thought they could manage the schooling only if they got some baby-sitting help. They hired a student named Wilma Deckard to live with them while they spent the summer studying at the conservatory.

Al moved to Chicago first, leaving Charlotte and Sonya at home. He lived in an eight-by-eight room at the YMCA on Wabash Avenue while he looked for an affordable apartment with a piano. The one he finally found, on the city's near north side, was upstairs over a laundry—"the hottest place I was ever in." The apartment was tiny, but it did have the piano, and it also had a small enclosed porch where Wilma could sleep. Sonya's bed was made up in a dresser drawer, which was pulled out and set up on two chairs every night.

Al spent the summer studying music theory and voice at the conservatory, and his voice teacher thought Al was slightly throaty. His exercise for correcting this was to have his student read aloud from the *Chicago Tribune* until the instructor struck a chord on the piano. Then Al was to sustain the note on whatever word he was reading at the time, finally running scales on it. One morning, he was reading along, waiting for the chord, when he came to a news story that said Purdue University had received federal support to build a music hall costing nearly $1.2 million. The construction was to be done by the Works Progress Administration.

Al managed not to choke on his words, but as soon as the lesson was over, he rushed outside to the nearest telephone and called Elliott's office. Elliott didn't even say hello. When his secretary told him who was on the line, he picked up the phone and chuckled: "Heh, heh! I thought you'd be calling. You better get your ass down here. I got you a million-dollar playhouse. I went to Washington because this country is being looted, and I thought I'd salvage some of the loot for Purdue."

There are various apocryphal stories about how Purdue got the federal money to build the Hall of Music, including one which claims that the money was approved for construction of an annex to the Administration Building— hence the bridge that connects the two buildings. Actually, Elliott told the committee controlling the funds that his was the only state university in the country that held regular large religious services on campus. When Purdue brought people like Bishop Fulton J. Sheen and Rev. Harry Emerson Fosdick to Fowler Hall, extra police and fire protection were needed, Elliott argued.

The president argued so successfully that he got enough money to build the largest theater in the country, one that was acoustically perfect, technologically state-of-the-art and large enough to accommodate administrative offices and rehearsal space for not only the musical organizations, but also one of the largest band units in the country.

That Elliott took such an active part in the creation of the Hall of Music was unusual. R. B. Stewart later would say that the project was Elliott's idea from the beginning. The president planned the building, lobbied for both the state and the federal money needed and personally went to Washington to close the deal. In January of 1958, the university's board of trustees would suspend its own rules, which prohibited naming a building for a living person. The trustees voted unanimously to rename the Hall of Music the Edward C. Elliott Hall of Music. Elliott, who was bedridden with the effects of a stroke at the time of the trustees' action, must have appreciated the rich irony of having the word *music* in the name of the university's tribute to his presidency. Al Stewart, whose efforts were more than indirectly responsible for the creation

This photo, taken at the Purdue Memorial Union in 1933, shows Charlotte dressed for a performance. She continued to sing with the Glee Club after graduating from Purdue.

Sonya was the apple of her father's eye as an infant and, years later, a mainstay of his musical organizations at Purdue.

of Elliott Hall, certainly appreciated the joke, as he recalled that vow never to spend a damn cent on music at Purdue.

The Elliott Hall of Music is immense by any standard. It boasts the largest seating capacity of any indoor theater in the United States—slightly more than Radio City Music Hall's. Today, with Purdue's enrollment in the 30,000-student range, Elliott Hall is remarkable, but in 1940, when it was completed, it was a marvel. The university had about 7,000 students then, which meant virtually all of them could sit down in the theater. To fully appreciate President Elliott's feat in acquiring the funding, we also have to recognize that Purdue of the late 1930s was still a comparatively obscure regional college which produced agriculturists, engineers and a few scientists. It had no music school, and never would have plans for one. In fact, Al Stewart had adopted as a kind of battle cry the slogan, Purdue, Where No Credit Is Given for Music, but Where Music Is a Distinct Credit to Purdue. Elliott eventually quibbled with Al about that choice of words.

"Listen son," he said. "The last time I checked, I was paying you a rather handsome salary, and we've got ourselves a pretty nice music hall. I'd call that giving some credit for music. Wouldn't you?" Al said he couldn't argue with the president's logic, and he duly rephrased his slogan, Where No *Academic* Credit Is Given... Elliott was satisfied.

The relationship between the president and the music director between 1931 and 1945, when Elliott retired, was unique. Elliott had what amounted to autocratic authority at Purdue throughout his presidency, and it could be argued that his beneficence "made" Al Stewart and the Purdue Musical Organizations. But the relationship was not one-sided—although there never was any doubt about who was in charge. The two men respected each other as preeminent in their respective fields, and Elliott built up the resources of P.M.O. not because he liked the sound of music, but because of the gains he perceived as coming to the university through Al's programs.

Late in his life, Elliott said that he had begun to respect Al on a day when their relationship almost ended. Shortly after the president had bequeathed his former office and other space in Fowler Hall to the musical organizations, he sent for Al, who recalls the audience this way:

Whenever Dr. Elliott admitted someone to his office, he always continued to read something, and this used to make me very uneasy. This time I was standing in front of his desk and finally, he peered up over his glasses and said, "Son, sit down." I sat down, and he went back to shuffling papers, not looking at me. Finally, he said: "I'm going to send you back to University Hall."

I was so startled that I blurted out, "Well, I'll be goddamned!"

He peered at me again over those glasses and said, "What's that? What did you say?"

I said, "I'm not at Purdue to go *back*—I'm here to go forward. If you want me to go back to University Hall, I'll leave, but I will *not* go back!"

I still didn't know what it was all about, but I thought I'd lost my job. I never expected to get away with talking to him like that, but I really was mad about being accused of something I knew nothing about. Finally, he said, "But there's been smoking in Fowler Hall."

"At my desk, yes, but there's been no smoking as far as the students are concerned."

He pulled a newspaper out from under his desk, and it was filled with cigarette butts. He said the janitor in Fowler had collected them and brought them over to the president's office.

I said, "Those were probably left by the canning company convention, which was just in Fowler. They were probably smoking out in the auditorium. I haven't got anything to do with the auditorium."

"The entire building is your responsibility," Dr. Elliott told me. I said nobody had ever told me that, and at this he shouted to Frank Hockema, the vice president who had an adjoining office. Frank came in and Dr. Elliott said, "Who is custodian of Fowler Hall?"

"Well," Frank said, "I guess I am. I don't think we ever changed it."

"I want it changed right now. Al, from now on, you're responsible for *anything* that goes on in Fowler Hall—the entire building."

I said, "Does that give me jurisdiction over the janitor?"

"Yes."

"Okay, if any janitor ever comes in here to tattle on me again, he's going to get fired!"

Dr. Elliott referred to that conversation many times after that. He said I was the only staff member who ever swore at him. It embarrassed me when he talked about it, because I felt terrible about it.

The Elliott Hall of Music boasts the largest seating capacity of any indoor theater in the United States, with slightly more seats than Radio City Music Hall.

In January of 1958, Purdue's board of trustees suspended its own rules, which prohibited naming a building for a living person, and voted unanimously to rename the Hall of Music the Edward C. Elliott Hall of Music.

This group of Glee Club singers gathered in the Hall of Music before a performance in the late 1940s. Seated left to right are William McCain, Horace Tyler, Wendell Swartz and Jack High. Standing are William Bugh, Darrell Ewbank and Robert Tam.

For all the fear and respect he inspired, Elliott did not take the authority of his office as seriously as others did. He later told Al he would have appreciated more back talk from the people who worked for him. "When I was a boy," Elliott said, "I used to hold the horses while my father shoed them. I could look a man in the eye and call him a son of a bitch. I thought I could run a university like that, but I was wrong. People should have talked back to me the way you did when I used those tactics."

Part of Elliott's charm was a wry sense of humor lurking beneath his gruff exterior. On one occasion, Elliott and Al were invited to the closing meeting of the American Institute of Cooperation, which held its national meeting at Purdue. "They spent about three days bragging about their great achievements," Al recalled, "and Dr. Elliott and I talked on the way over about how this was a group that seemed terribly pleased with itself."

Al was asked to lead the assembly in singing "Blest Be the Tie That Binds Our Hearts in Christian Love" and "God Be with You Till We Meet Again." Elliott then was to lead a closing prayer to end the meeting. At the end of the singing, the president—a practicing, but not openly pious Episcopalian—looked around and said, very slowly, "Dear God, send us all home and make us as great as we *think* we are."

On another occasion, Elliott sent for Al and told him: "The excise boys are coming to raid the fraternities tonight."

Al wasn't sure what the president expected of him. Finally, he said, "Well, I know I work for you, but I hope you don't expect me to be a stool pigeon."

"We both take a drink, but not in church," Elliott retorted. "There's a law against the boys drinking in the fraternity houses."

That afternoon, Al called the Interfraternity Council president, and by dinnertime every house on campus was dry as dust. "He *knew* I would do that," Al said. "That's what he wanted, but of course, he couldn't say so."

Another person who wasn't awed by Elliott was his own secretary. Helen Hand was a tall, big-boned woman, eight years older than her boss. Her gray, wispy hair usually was out of place, and her standard attire was a black, ankle-length skirt and a white blouse. "I never saw her in anything else," Al remembered. Every payday, she would call Al on the telephone when his check was ready and announce it with the words, "Young man, this is the day the eagle flies." Once when Al asked Elliott about having the pipe organ in Fowler Hall repaired, the president sent for his secretary.

"Miss Hand," he said, when she had come in, "what the hell's the matter with that damned organ? It's left testicle is out again!"

Miss Hand said she would look into it and returned to her desk, but when Al left the president, he found the secretary furious and itching to confront Elliott alone. "No young whippersnapper is going to talk to *me* like that!" she raged. "I've worked for *three* presidents."

Chapter 9

Al Stewart directs a World War II era performance at the Purdue Memorial Union. Some of the singers are in military uniform.

CHANGES ON THE HOME FRONT

While the Purdue Musical Organizations were growing in off-campus prestige and on-campus status, social and musical changes were occurring in America which would serve to confirm the wisdom of Al's decision to make the Men's Glee Club his headliner. After initially offering instrumental music almost exclusively, the big bands which dominated the popular music of the late 1930s began to feature more vocalists, both as soloists and in groups. The relentless approach of World War II brought a new status to the American military and with it an appreciation for male group singing. The Varsity Glee Club was in demand to sing for ever more prestigious audiences. Large corporations and national organizations invited the Purdue men to cities around the Midwest. They sang for conventions, religious services, board meetings and banquets, and they never failed to impress. Al Stewart directed them with an economy of movement that belied the fire with which they sang. A four-year veteran of the Glee Club later would explain: "His hands and the baton—when he used one—were employed strictly for the sake of the audience. He really directed us with his eyes." And indeed, when his young men were performing, Al faced them, back to the audience, barely moving, but looking into their souls, daring them to miss a cue or hold a note a fraction of a second too long.

By the time the new Hall of Music was ready in 1940, the Glee Club was a group worthy of such an arena. The nucleus of the ensemble that would take Purdue to national fame in Fred Waring's Carnegie Hall extravaganza was in place already, and the musical organizations were ready to help Purdue do its part in the war effort's home front. World War II would change Purdue forever. There were short-term and long-term effects. First there was the drastic reduction in the number of young men on campus as enlistments and the draft drained away students and faculty alike. Later, there was an influx of men in uniform, as the various services used Purdue and other universities to help train officers and specialists. Missing no opportunity, Al would organize military glee clubs, which sang in uniform. Government-funded "temporary" buildings were thrown together to meet the needs of these programs. Some of these structures would still be in place forty years later. Finally, when the war was won and the G.I.'s had come home, college enrollments would swell to unprecedented levels. Not only did the advantages of the G.I. bill make a college education too good a bargain to pass up, but the war had taught Americans to respect technology. Great strides in communication and aviation had brought the rest of the world closer to an America that had done its best to remain isolationist during the 1930s. It also had brought women out of the home, into the workplace, and it had opened their eyes to new possibilities. All these changes would affect Al Stewart and his singers.

One of the first things Al did was start worrying. A music director in his early thirties was by no means exempt from the draft during the greatest mobilization in the country's history. Although he was ready to serve, he didn't want to find himself as a buck private in the front lines, so he considered enlisting. However, President Elliott urged him to stay, telling him not to worry about the draft. Early in the war, Al was offered a commission in the Army Special Services, but Elliott asked him to turn it down. Later, the navy asked him to accept a commission to direct the Blue Jacket Choir at the Great Lakes Naval Base. Again, he went to Elliott, arguing that he couldn't afford to turn down another commission if he were going to end up an enlisted man with very narrow options.

This time Elliott said, "I didn't plan to tell you, but I have a letter on file from General Hershey (head of the Selective Service), which lists the names of people on campus who are of draft age but who are considered essential here. Your name is in the letter and Hershey has signed it. You aren't going to be drafted. Now get to work."

Charlotte and Al outside their first home soon after their marriage. They eventually lived in twelve different houses in various neighborhoods.

The young Stewart in an intense moment during a performance on campus. Many of his singers insist he directed mostly with his eyes.

So Al fought World War II on the stage, leading war bond rallies and putting on shows designed to keep up the morale of both civilians and the hundreds of servicemen on campus. One of the war bond rallies was arranged after a call from Rudy Vallee. The singer wanted to include Purdue on a patriotic tour. Vallee would accept no fee, since the tour was part of his contribution to the war effort. The catch was that the Purdue rally would have to be on a Sunday. "In those days," Al said, "we did not do anything—and I mean *nothing*—on a Sunday at Purdue."

After failing to talk Vallee's representative into another day, Al went to see the president. "I wanted to persuade him that this would be such a great thing for the campus, having a big star like Rudy Vallee here. We would attract a lot of people, and it would be a real shot in the arm for spirit and morale."

Elliott was skeptical. "I don't like to do anything like this on Sunday," he said, but Al persisted, arguing that the contribution to the war effort would be significant, that the motivation for the show made it more than just entertainment.

Finally Elliott weakened. "Could you guarantee that there would be nothing out of line, nothing on the program that would embarrass the university?" he asked.

Of course Al could, although he had only heard Vallee sing on records. He never had attended one of his shows, and the one at Purdue turned out to be on the risqué side by 1942 standards. Thirty minutes into the entertainment, the president of the university rose and marched out of the Hall of Music. "I was deeply embarrassed," Al said. "For six weeks after that I avoided Dr. Elliott. If I saw him coming across campus, I'd head in another direction. If I knew he was going to be at a party, I wouldn't go. I was afraid to face him because I knew what he'd say—and I had it coming. It finally wore off, and he never said anything about it. I was embarrassed as hell, but I was still glad we had that show."

The Vallee production had a positive effect on campus morale, but the rapid turnover of people and students' uncertainty about their own futures were constant negative factors. In the spring of 1943, Elliott asked Al if he could come up with something that would improve spirits on campus. Al's response was to play a kind of musical joke on the university. He promoted a concert with posters and ads featuring only a large question mark and a time for an event in the Hall of Music. With a full house assembled for the Question Mark Convocation, Al appeared alone on stage. From behind the closed curtains, a rousing rendition of "Hail Purdue" began, and as the 6,000 people stood, the curtain opened, and there—alone on the huge stage—was a tiny pedestal and on it a phonograph playing the fight song. As the number finished, Al walked over and snapped off the phonograph, and the confused audience sat down.

Still alone on stage, Al told the crowd about his great secret fear: That he would forget about a show and find himself facing an audience with nothing prepared. "I guess that's what happened tonight," he said. He proposed solving the problem by using volunteers from the audience. "We've got some chairs back there, and maybe we can fill them up and get something going and still put on a show." The "volunteers" were called by number, and each would go backstage for a chair, then bring it onstage. To the apparently confused crowd of students milling about with chairs or sitting self-consciously onstage, were added a handful of audience members who hadn't been called, but who wanted to help out.

With about one hundred people finally seated, a piano was pushed out, and when Al brought his hand down, the first notes from the singers told the crowd that this was an exceedingly well drilled group of "volunteers." "Those poor souls who'd come up to help out felt silly as the devil," Al said. "They'd get up and sneak off one at a time, and the audience was just yelling! They knew, of course, that it was a put-up job. We had something to talk about for a while after that."

Events like the Question Mark Convocation provided not only a campus chuckle but a sense of community. They also added to Al Stewart's growing reputation as a showman and a character. He was brash, daring and unpredictable, and he didn't mind if a few people thought he was *too* flamboyant. Elliott had given his music director a clear mandate, and Al was delighted to

Al Stewart and the P.M.O. officers got together for this business meeting in 1944. Seated left to right are Assistant Director Joseph Ragains, Alphonso Kwasnieski, Mary Lou Hole, Peter Smith (Pete Kelley), Al Stewart, Henry Ryder, Sandy Wolin, Doree Martin and Bill Kennedy. Standing is P.M.O. staff member Vassie Durnell.

Bruce G. "Mickey" McGuire came to Purduc from a World War II hitch in the Pacific and fell in love with the music. A tenor soloist with the Glee Club, he was manager of the group in 1946–47.

As assistant director to Al Stewart in 1969, Mickey McGuire was credited with making P.M.O. run smoothly. Besides helping with musical direction, he made sure that every booking was handled in a professional manner. Al called Mickey "absolutely the most unselfish person I've ever met."

use it: "The president told me anybody who had any complaints about me could call him. He said that would stop about 85 percent of them, and he said to tell the other 15 percent to go to hell."

Purdue in the early 1940s was a campus full of men in uniform. One day in 1944, one of them approached Al after a Glee Club concert in the Purdue Memorial Union. Al remembers the meeting this way: "He was just about the handsomest young fellow I'd ever seen. He said he had just come in from the Pacific and heard our show, and he thought it was just about the greatest thing he'd ever heard, and he wanted to know if there was some way he could be a part of it."

Mickey McGuire was a part of P.M.O.'s team for more than three decades after that, first as a Glee Club member and then as Al's most trusted assistant. Mickey would become the man who freed Al from the endless details of running a student organization that has to make a professional appearance at all times. "He was just a good everything," Al said, "and he is absolutely the most unselfish person I've ever met. Mickey never thought about credit for himself."

Mickey McGuire had studied to be a Baptist minister, but Purdue became his true vocation. During his student days, he quietly absorbed every detail of Al's directing style. "When Mickey directed, he did everything exactly as I would," Al said. "Anybody else would put something of their own into a number, but Mickey could do it exactly like me." This meant that Al had a director who could fill in at rehearsals or performances of the Glee Club. Mickey also could take responsibility for any of the other groups, and he directed most of them for various periods throughout his career. But his greatest value to Al Stewart was that he thought of everything. With Mickey on his team, Al didn't have to worry about travel arrangements or equipment or wardrobes or any of the other considerations that are routine until someone forgets one. Mickey never forgot.

When it came to handling people, Al recalls that Mickey surpassed even him in some situations:

> He could talk anybody into anything. He'd turn on that charm and people would just melt. I remember getting to this restaurant for a show, and we

told the manager we needed the piano up on the stage. He said they couldn't do it; there was no one to move it. There were all these waiters around, but he said they couldn't touch the piano because of union rules.

I just walked out and left that to Mickey. If I stayed there and argued, I'd just get mad and nothing would get accomplished. So I left, and twenty minutes later I came back, and there were all the waiters, huffing and puffing around the piano. Anybody who runs an organization like P.M.O. needs a guy like Mickey.

No one else worked for Al as long as Mickey did, but the various people he hired over the decades contributed to the growth of the musical programs, because Al tended to hire them for their specialized talents. Rosemary Robinson Funk started as an accompanist in 1934 and was affiliated with Al for more than fifty years. Bill Luhman and John Farley were outstanding pianists and arrangers; Marvin Meyers became the full-time assistant director of extension music programs in counties throughout the state; Jack Young was hired for his promotion and fund-raising abilities; Dick Smith had learned to direct as a Glee Club member; Byron Fox, according to Al, was "second only to Mickey as a right-handed helper to a left-handed director"; and Bill Allen joined the staff because Al—approaching retirement—saw the need for an individual with both talent and a solid formal music education.

Chapter 10

Under Al's leadership, Victory Varieties consistently drew big-name talent to Purdue. Singers Barbara McNair and Jimmy Dean were among the headliners for a 1964 Victory Varieties performance. Behind them in this photo are Al and West Lafayette hotel manager Paul Williams.

VICTORY VARIETIES

In 1943, if you were going to name something—a park, a street, a stadium, a dog, or a stage production—you couldn't go wrong with *Victory*. America's war machine was going into high gear after some demoralizing setbacks early in World War II. Now a national single-mindedness prevailed. The country focused all its energies on whipping the Axis powers. *Victory* was a national password, and when Al Stewart got the idea to bring big-name entertainment to the Purdue campus, the name came naturally.

Victory Varieties would last for a quarter of a century, and it would bring the most popular entertainers in the country to West Lafayette. "I had the idea that Purdue could be an oasis," Al explained. "We had this great Hall of Music, and it was a marvelous place to work. I always liked popular music. I bugged R. B. Stewart [vice president and treasurer] about it for about a year. Finally, he said, 'I'll give you $1,500. If you lose that, that's the end of it.' That's when I said one of the smartest things I ever said. I told him, 'Okay, but if we make anything, we'll put it back into entertainment facilities for the university. It won't go for anything else.' R. B. didn't think we had a chance to make any money, so he went for it."

Al was in the Hall of Music vestibule counting the house the night of the first Victory Varieties, October 23, 1943. A little more than 2,000 people showed up to see Milt Britton and Bonnie Baker, and R. B. Stewart was impressed enough to offer some more seed money. A month later, the Vagabonds headlined the second show. The following year Victory Varieties was off and running with three shows, including one featuring Les Brown and His Band of Renown. "The momentum just built," Al said. "We tried to do everything first-class, and it spread by word of mouth among the entertainers that Purdue was a great place to play. They liked the Hall of Music, they liked the fact that we didn't try to exploit them while they were here, and they liked that full house with all those seats."

When World War II ended, no one wanted to change the name of something that had been so successful, but it was easy enough to apply *Victory* to athletic teams. Most of the shows were scheduled to conform to home football weekends. As the series gathered strength, entertainers began to do more than one show. Two performances were routine, and four were not unusual. Bob Hope, at the peak of his stardom in 1949, did four shows in a two-day visit in March.

The lineup of Victory Varieties stars is a Who's Who of popular music and comedy from the forties, fifties, and sixties. It includes Frank Sinatra, Danny Kaye, Gene Krupa, Fred Waring, Vaughn Monroe, Tommy Dorsey, Duke Ellington, Ed Sullivan, Rosemary Clooney, Jack Benny, Johnny Mathis, the Kingston Trio, Simon and Garfunkel, Bob Hope, Bill Cosby and dozens of others.

"The only big name we didn't get was Bing Crosby," Al claimed. "He wanted to come, and we wanted him here, but we couldn't agree on the money. He insisted that his check be made out to a charity, and we had a policy against doing benefits. He was stubborn, and we were stubborn, and we just never could get it resolved. Of course, Bob Hope was telling him what a great place Purdue was to play, so I think he wanted to do a show here."

Most of the bookings for Victory Varieties were handled by Arthur Goldsmith, who headed Paramount Attractions, a Chicago entertainment agency. Al had met Goldsmith through Bert Loeb, a Lafayette merchant. Goldsmith, a big-city Jew whose father had been a theatrical agent, and Stewart, the son of a small-town Methodist minister, were an unlikely team, and their relationship was punctuated by occasional disagreements, but both understood middle-of-the-road entertainment. They adjusted to the evolution of popular music throughout the lifetime of Victory Varieties.

Only rock-and-roll acts do not appear in large numbers on the Varieties pantheon. Some of these—like the Beach Boys and Jose Feliciano—were booked after their appeal broadened enough to draw the kinds of audiences

Al was aiming for. "We booked the shows with the idea that the audience would be 51 percent townspeople and faculty and 49 percent students, although the students never made 49 percent."

A committee of Purdue staff members operated Victory Varieties. The personnel changed occasionally over the years, but Al, as chairman, and John Ditamore, as director of the Hall of Music, served continuously.

With Victory Varieties in its heyday, campus weekends were eventful, and plenty of money flowed into the local economy. An alumnus who drove in with his family might have dinner and see Bob Hope's show on Friday night, check out of his motel in time for the football game Saturday and eat dinner in a Lafayette restaurant on the way home. The visiting celebrities could treat themselves to a weekend of Midwest hospitality and, for some, the chance to act like everyday people was a welcome change. Al shielded his famous guests from the public as much as possible. He organized private parties in various local hotels and, for a while, at the Lafayette Country Club. A Bob Hope or a Fred Waring could relax there and have a meal and a drink without being introduced to a succession of autograph seekers. He might even be sung to or sing along with Purdue's Glee Club. Although Al had an unbreakable rule against using the Glee Club—or any other amateur act in a Victory Varieties show, the student singers often were included in social events where they got a chance to get to know the visiting celebrities.

As for Al and Charlotte's daughters, Sonya and Joanna, they were almost in their teens before they found out that most households *didn't* have regular visits from people like Jack Benny and Patti Page. When Sonya (now Mrs. John R. Eddy) was a Purdue sophomore, she was perturbed one Saturday in 1957 when her father asked her to entertain one of his guests at the football game. Sonya had other plans, which she didn't want to cancel. That is, until she learned that the guest was Pat Boone, who was scheduled to sing at the Hall of Music that night. "I was in the kitchen arguing with Dad, and America's latest dreamboat was sitting in the living room waiting for me," Sonya said. Boone was a teen heartthrob, but not yet a Victory Varieties headliner. Al had run into him at the airport that day but hadn't recognized him.

(*Inset*) The famous Stewart smile was at its best in this photo, taken in his Hall of Music office during the 1940s.

Three generations of the Stewart family were present for this singing portrait. Left to right are Sonya; Al's mother, Ethel Pearson Stewart; Charlotte; Al; and younger daughter, Joanna.

Al Stewart is flanked by Jerry Colonna and Bob Hope in this photo taken at a post-performance party at the Lafayette Country Club. Hope and Colonna both directed and sang with the Glee Club at the party.

Al Stewart and Dinah Shore got together after the Glee Club and the popular singer shared a program in Detroit.

Jack Benny enjoyed visiting the Stewart home during his trips to Purdue. At left in this photo is Bob Friend, major league pitching star and brother of Charlotte Stewart.

Louis "Satchmo" Armstrong starred on a Victory Varieties program in 1966. Behind him are Al Stewart, hotel manager Paul Williams and Hall of Music director John Ditamore.

Singing great Nat King Cole earned his Purdue letter during a Victory Varieties visit in 1963.

A battered violin hangs on a wall in the Stewart living room. Scratched on it is the message, "To Al with much fun—Jack Benny." The comedian made the violin a gift after he spent a relaxed Saturday with the Stewart family eating bacon and eggs, talking about show business and being a private man instead of a personality. The instrument was a prop, Al explained. "Whenever he was going to do his violin routine, he'd say something about wanting the violin, and a prop man would slide it from the wings across the stage. That's why the back is all marked up. He said he wanted to give me something, so he gave me a prop violin."

Younger daughter Joanna (now Mrs. James B. McNeely), who was an infant when Robert Goulet spent an hour romping on the floor with her, recalls that celebrity visits were simply taken for granted by her and her sister. "I think that's why those people liked to come here. No one made a big fuss about anybody. Of course we *knew* when somebody was famous, but we were just so used to it that things were always relaxed. And of course, Dad wasn't awed by anyone."

It's true that there probably wasn't a person alive whom Al Stewart wouldn't tell to go to hell if the direction were appropriate. However, he took a childlike delight in meeting celebrities, and he never stopped being filled with wonder at the discovery of down-to-earth qualities in the most distinguished entertainers. During a Victory Varieties visit, comedian Danny Kaye sat in Al's office on a Saturday afternoon talking about the pride he had in his craft. "You know," Kaye said, "I could take the next student who walks by here and spend a half hour teaching him some routines. Then he could go out on the stage and have an audience in stitches for fifteen minutes—they'd love him. But they'd hate him tomorrow, because he'd have to use dirty material. That's the only way he could get laughs, because he has no talent. Since I've been blessed with talent, I don't have to degrade myself that way. I will never use dirty material to get a laugh."

The story delighted Al because it not only showed Kaye's professionalism, but it reaffirmed the basic values that Al tried to build into his entertainment.

During one show, Al got into a backstage discussion with singer Ginny Simms when the two of them discovered that they were serving on Presbyterian pulpit committees that were competing to hire the same minister—he in West Lafayette and she in Beverly Hills. They argued so vehemently that the singer missed her introduction. "Many people think entertainers have no depth, but here was one of the most glamorous women in the country, so concerned about her church that she forgot about a show she was doing," Al marveled. *"No depth?"*

The success of Victory Varieties performed the unlikely feat of making Purdue exactly the kind of show business oasis Al had envisioned when he created it. It made celebrities aware of Purdue, and it led to bonuses for Al and his singers, like a 1956 trip to Alaska to entertain U.S. troops with Bob Hope. The star-studded entourage included, besides Hope, Mickey Mantle, Ginger Rogers, Jerry Colonna and Hedda Hopper. When Al met the famous Hollywood gossip columnist, he told her she was a disappointment. "My wife has sillier hats than that," he said.

During a Varieties weekend headlined by Eddie Cantor, Al was approached by a young man who identified himself as a protégé of Cantor's. "But I never get to do anything," he complained. "Could I get one number of the show?" Al turned him down, explaining his no-amateurs policy, but the singer persisted in his argument and finally won out. "Eddy Fisher turned out to be pretty good," Al chuckled.

Al believed there were two important elements that made Victory Varieties successful. The first had to do with the way entertainers were booked. "We never used a packaged show," he said. "We wouldn't buy a headliner who came with a dog act, a pony act, a magician and a tap-dancing girl. We booked every single act separately. We would get the star first and then assemble the rest of the show. Sure you have secondary acts, and maybe somebody we thought was a comer, but there were no fillers. That way, we got entertainers who were going all out, and sometimes we ended up with more than one headliner on the same show."

The second important element, Al thought, was the way ticket sales were handled. "The secret, the real secret," he insisted, "along with the fact that we never let the audience down, was that we never announced a show ahead of

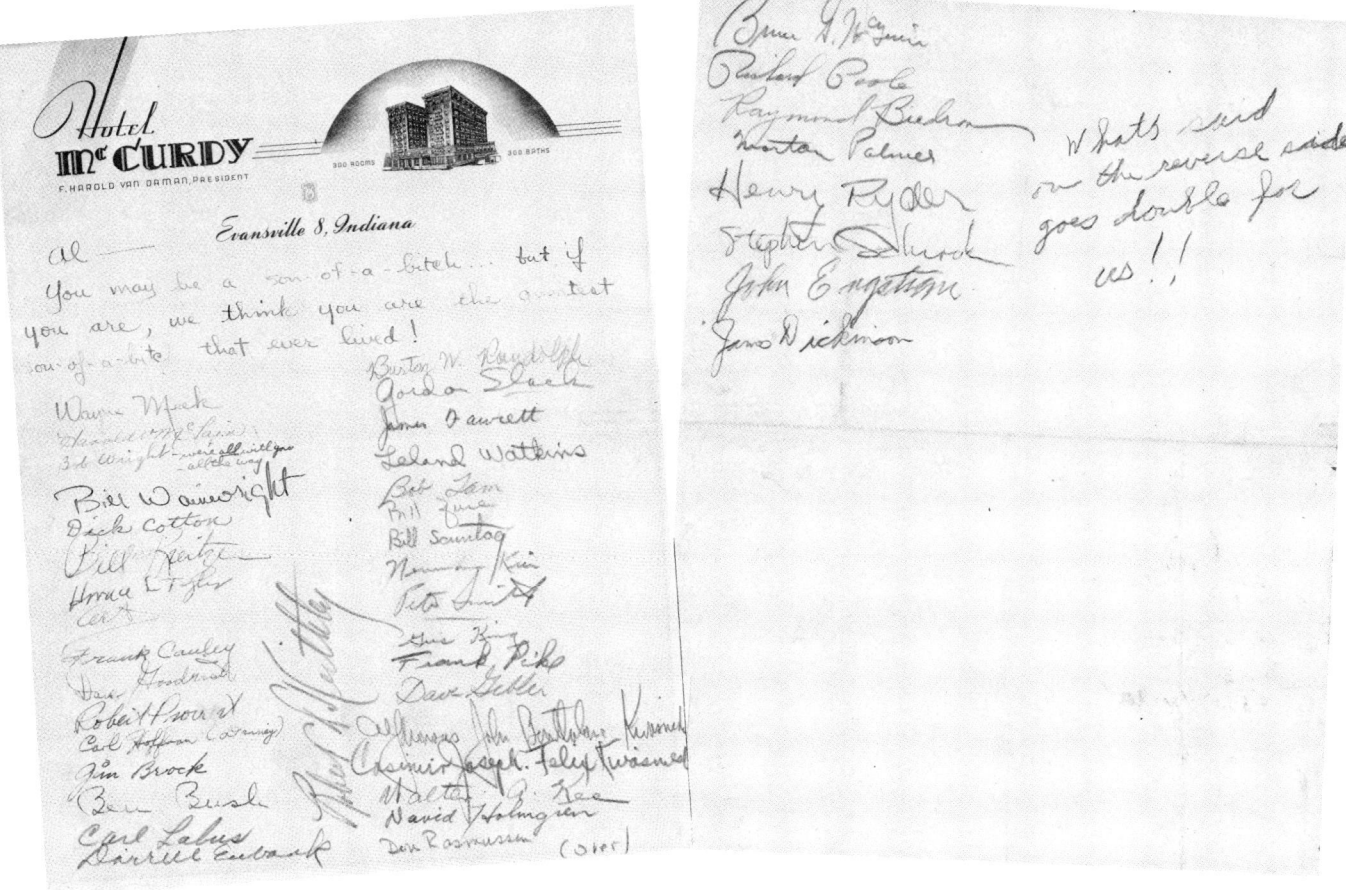

In 1946, Al Stewart, saying he was "tired of being a son of a bitch," considered leaving Purdue to accept another job offer. Members of the Glee Club convinced him to stay with this letter.

time. If we had football games on consecutive Saturdays, we wouldn't announce the show for the second Saturday until the first show was going on. Every agency would say to me, 'It's impossible to run a theater like that.' I'd say, 'It sure is, but we're doing it!' You see, I didn't want people picking and choosing. If I announced three shows to be put on in a month, people would say they couldn't afford all three of them, so they'd pick this one or that. But if I could get them in the theater, and show them a great time, they'd be afraid to miss the next one. A lot of the shows would sell out the night I announced them."

Not every Victory Varieties production was a hit. Dean Martin and Jerry Lewis, before they became the hottest comedy act in the country, did a money-losing show. "They put on a fine show," Al recalled, "but nobody had heard of them, and we couldn't sell them. Six months later everybody was begging me to bring them in. People didn't even know they'd been here." Another failure was an unusual appearance by composer-pianist Igor Stravinsky with Woody Herman's band. Al respected Herman as a great innovator and the first big-band leader to play modern jazz, but the Stravinsky appearance was too much for the audience. "He came out with this wild hair, and people thought he was going to do a comedy act," Al said. "Hell, they were walking out in the middle of the performance. I was really embarrassed, but we just weren't ready for that here."

When one Victory Varieties show did poorly, Al came up with an ingenious way to needle the people who stayed home. He announced that a ticket stub from the low-grossing show would get the holder preference in buying seats for the next show, which turned out to be Bob Hope's first Purdue appearance. "People would set their alarms for three o'clock in the morning and call me, madder than hell. Everybody claimed that was the only show they'd ever missed."

The phenomenal success of the Victory Varieties continued into the late 1960s, when changing musical tastes and a restive student body began to demand a different kind of entertainment. "The student groups wanted to bring in a lot of loud rock music, and I didn't want anything to do with it,"

Al said. "I told President Hovde I was either resigning from the Varieties committee or from the university. I quit as the chairman, and the thing folded."

The loss of the Victory Varieties was one of the great disappointments of Al's career, but he never considered trying to bring it back. "You just couldn't do it. Television has made the prices of entertainers so ridiculous that we'd have to charge $100 a ticket. It was a great thing at the time, and if we'd kept it, it might still work, but you'll never see anything like it again."

Chapter 11

When wartime mobilization drained manpower resources and placed many college men under travel restrictions, Al made the Purduettes his headliner group. The first Purduettes, with Doree Martin seated at the piano, are pictured in this 1943 photograph. Martin later became successful in popular music.

SIRENS IN WHITE SATIN

When America goes to war, its music goes with it. Popular songs of the 1940s did not have the militaristic ring of World War I era music, but they reflected the nation's commitment in more subtle ways. Songs like "I'll Be Seeing You in All the Old Familiar Places," "I'll Be Home for Christmas" and "Don't Sit under the Apple Tree" expressed America's concern for the boys overseas. The U. S. government understood the value of music to troop and national morale, and it created the largest special services organization in history to provide entertainment for the troops and to help raise money to finance the war. Musical celebrities like Glenn Miller cheerfully donned uniforms and made their music under the auspices of the War Department. Miller strung together jazzed-up versions of traditional marches and made a hit record out of "American Patrol."

Another effect of the war was increased popularity of men's choral music. Psychologically, the sound of a well-disciplined men's singing group fit in well with the nation's commitment to its fighting men. Al Stewart had put together perhaps the best amateur men's choral group in the country during the late 1930s and early 1940s, but he wasn't really able to capitalize on the demand for the Glee Club's services. The trip to Carnegie Hall in May 1942—six months after the Japanese attack on Pearl Harbor—was a temporary last hurrah for the group.

By the time classes resumed in the fall, the male population of Purdue had been drastically depleted, as the military mobilization swept up an entire generation of young men. Many of those who stayed and all of those who came later for education related to their military assignments were subject to travel restrictions, which forbade them from leaving the immediate area. Al still had a Men's Glee Club, but he couldn't take them on the road. His headliner was grounded, and Purdue had no singing ambassadors. None of the other P.M.O. groups, as they existed at the time, could produce the impact of the Glee Club. Al decided he needed something new.

Obviously, the new group had to be women, but the traditional choir—while fine for certain groups and occasions—wouldn't work for a lot of the bookings the Glee Club had been getting. Al wanted something upbeat, sassy and sexy—a whole stage full of Anita O'Days. Thus were born the Purduettes, thirteen Purdue coeds picked for their "musical ability, looks and personality," plus any show business experience they could bring to the job.

"Actually, I had been kicking around the idea of a female group like that for a long time," Al said. "The war restrictions just forced me do something about it. I still preferred a men's group—always will—but the Purduettes were my headliner for the rest of the war, and they didn't do us any harm."

Al had four costumes designed for the Purduettes, and these ranged from sexy white satin, off-the-shoulder formals to saintly black-and-white choir gowns. With this group, as with any other, Al insisted that every audience had to be treated differently: "I don't care how good you are. You're going to bomb if you don't give the audience what it comes to hear. If I put those girls in front of some ladies' church group and had them singing cute little love songs in their low-cut dresses, I'd probably get myself fired, but I can do that material for an alumni club or some men's group in Chicago. For those ladies, we had to do some hymns, but we could do those, too."

With their upbeat style and good looks, the Purduettes were an instant hit. Among their first bookings were a state loan company convention in Indianapolis and a district Rotary Club convention. An article in a Rotary publication enthused: "Some girls! The prettiest things I ever saw in one bunch in my life . . . and they can sing, too!"

Al took the girl group on an eastern tour, which climaxed with a performance at the Eastman Kodak Company in Rochester, New York. They were good enough to receive preliminary inquiries from commercial radio stations interested in developing a show around them.

The Purduettes of 1945. Al Stewart established the women's group as P.M.O.'s headliner when World War II restrictions and manpower shortages impaired the all-male Varsity Glee Club.

The Purduettes of 1961 were dressed differently but just as attractively as their counterparts of the forties.

By the mid-1960s, the Purduettes had become a much larger organization—almost three times the size of the original group of thirteen.

(*Right*) These pretty Purduettes are Bobbie Preston, Connie Caadd and Jayne Gaylord.

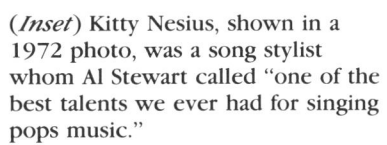

(*Inset*) Kitty Nesius, shown in a 1972 photo, was a song stylist whom Al Stewart called "one of the best talents we ever had for singing pops music."

The Purduettes of 1980.

Although the Purduettes were about as wholesome in appearance, manners and performing material as it is possible for a group of healthy young women to be, Al received some public criticism from people who thought the group was on the suggestive side. His standard reply was, "I hope my own daughters grow up to be as nice as these girls are." In fact, both his daughters did become Purduettes, Sonya in the late 1950s and Joanna in the early 1960s.

One of the original members of the Purduettes was one of the most talented performers ever to belong to the musical organizations. Dorothy "Doree" Martin was a soloist, the group's piano accompanist and a facile composer and arranger as well—good enough that she wanted to take a shot at a show business career. She withdrew from Purdue and, with an enthusiastic P.M.O. send-off, set out for New York, where she hoped to sell her songs. She met not so much failure as frustration, finding that the doors to Tin Pan Alley just weren't open to an unknown girl with no connections. She returned to the Midwest, working professionally as a vocalist and pianist for several years before taking another crack at a songwriting career, this time on the west coast. Her second effort was more successful. In the late 1950s, her song "Sixteen Reasons" caught the fancy of teenagers, and it became a hit record of the early rock-and-roll era.

Although Al restored the Men's Glee Club to top billing as soon as the war was over, the Purduettes added a new and permanent dimension to the Purdue Musical Organizations. For a short time, he changed the name to the Choraleers, but the group's peppy style of delivering solid choral music shows never changed. In the structure of P.M.O. today, the Purduettes are the group of choice for many audiences.

Chapter 12

The 1950s opened the Golden Age of P.M.O., when the Varsity Glee Club established an international reputation as singing ambassadors for the United States. The 1950 Glee Club is pictured.

THE GOLDEN AGE OF P.M.O.

At the end of the school year in 1945, Edward Elliott retired as president of Purdue. On his last day in office, he called Al Stewart and asked him to come to the president's office at 4:30 p.m. Al recalls:

> When I got there, there was not a thing on his desk except a single piece of paper, lying facedown. He said, "Al, you're the only one on my staff who ever swore at me." I said, "Please don't remind me of that, Dr. Elliott. I was young and very foolish then."
>
> He picked up the paper on his desk and said, "This is your contract," and he tore it in about six pieces. I thought for a minute I'd lost my job, but he had that glint in his eye, and he looked at me over his glasses, then reached down and got another paper out of his drawer. "This is the largest raise I'm allowed to give without action from the Board of Trustees," he said. I think it was about $1,500 a year—a lot of money in those days. He told me to sign it and then he put it facedown on his desk. He got up, reached back to get his hat and put it on his head, threw his arm over my shoulder and said, "Come on, let's go." And we walked out together.

It was Elliott's last act as president of Purdue.

Elliott's departure ended an era for Al Stewart, and a new era was about to begin for Purdue as well. The war in Europe already was over, and final victory was just a matter of weeks away. Within a year, the return of America's fighting men, along with liberal educational benefits for veterans, would spill people onto the nation's college campuses in unprecedented numbers. Purdue was no exception, and the university was nearly overwhelmed by its own enrollment increases. Educationally and logistically, the institution faced a difficult adjustment period, but musically it would be a golden age.

"There's no question," Al affirmed, "that the late forties and early fifties glee clubs were the best I had."

This difference had nothing to do with talent or experience or leadership. It was purely a matter of maturity. The throats in a college glee club typically are eighteen to twenty-two years old. Now they ranged up into the late twenties and occasionally the early thirties. Men, instead of boys. The basses were deeper, the baritones more mellow, the tenors clearer. The results were magnificent.

Musical tastes also remained favorable for the Glee Club, and Purdue still was basking in the glory of the 1942 triumph in New York. Al Stewart's reputation had spread, and the performances of those postwar years only enhanced it. One of the shows would be so good that it would change the life of a Glee Club member.

J. Peter Smith had spent one semester at Purdue studying engineering before he was called into the army to serve on the European front. During that semester he had decided that he had no future in engineering, but he had also sung with the Glee Club and had what he considered "a remarkable experience," despite the fact that in his first solo number before an audience, he forgot the words to "The Lost Chord." "I could have died," he said. Al's reaction to that initial failure was "very kind, very supportive," Smith said, and because of that, the young singer's confidence on stage grew.

"When the war was over, I decided I wanted to come back and sing for Al Stewart, but I didn't know what I wanted to study." Smith went to see Al and asked for his advice. "I said, 'What can I study while singing for you?'" Al recommended a program in industrial physical education, and Smith eventually was a member of the first class to get a Purdue degree in that discipline.

While he was a senior, Smith traveled to Chicago for the Glee Club's annual concert for the Indiana Society of Chicago, a large and influential organization. One of the society's members was Glen Hillis, an Indiana philanthropist, who made a practice of supporting the educations of promising young people. Hillis was so impressed with the Glee Club's performance that he resolved to sponsor a member in an entertainment career. After consulting with Purdue Vice President Frank Hockema and subsequently with Al, Hillis offered his sponsorship to Pete Smith.

Hillis first sent Smith to New York for an audition, which yielded a report that the young man had talent, but needed more formal training. Smith graduated from Purdue and, with Hillis paying the bills, enrolled in the Indiana University School of Music. Subsequently, still under his benefactor's financial wing, Smith went to New York and began a successful singing and acting career which included leading rolls in the Broadway musicals *South Pacific*, *Wish You Were Here* and *Two's Company,* all of which he appeared in under his professional name, Pete Kelley. "The name change was dictated by the Actors' Equity Union," Smith explains. "There can only be one person using a name at a time, and mine was already taken, so I used my mother's maiden name."

Now a successful talent agent in New York, Smith is deeply grateful for the opportunity his Glee Club experience brought him and fiercely proud of the way music is treated at Purdue. "We did it without any school of music, and we did it better than just about anybody else," he says. "Al always talks about No Fun without Music and No Music without Fun, but that wasn't just a slogan. That's the way we lived it." Like many P.M.O. veterans, Smith has fond memories: of sleeping in luggage racks on bus trips; of learning to play bridge with Henry Ryder, now a Purdue trustee; and of appearing in revived Harlequin productions, which became a joint effort of P.M.O. and the campus theater group of the era. "I was singing 'Desert Song' one night and I tripped on my sword—almost fell in the orchestra pit."

The 1950s began on a high note for the Glee Club when the U. S. State Department sponsored a six-week European tour during which the Purdue singers became not only overseas ambassadors, but instruments in the rebuilding of friendly relations between the United States and Germany. As with most official invitations, this one was the idea of the invitee. Al had been intrigued by the potential for such a trip, and he approached U. S. Representative Charles Halleck about it. Halleck, an influential congressman from Rensselaer, Indiana, who died in 1986, persuaded the State Department that the trip was valuable to American interests, and he helped secure the funding.

The tour included stops in Paris and Luxembourg, where the Glee Club met Perle Mesta, then the U.S. ambassador to the tiny nation. Al had been warned that she was extremely rigorous about etiquette and would insist on being called "madame." Instead, she came traipsing through the grass of the runway where the Glee Club plane touched down and insisted on being introduced to and chatting with every boy.

The main focus of the European trip was a tour of German universities and cities, where rubble still lay in bombed-out streets, but where the people were surprisingly forthcoming. At a reception after a concert, a man approached Al and said, "Herr Director, would you exchange autographs?" Al agreed and wrote a friendly message on a piece of paper. The German man did the same, and when he handed the note to Al, it read, "When I heard the Purdue Glee Club sing, I was made homesick for the land I learned to love while I was a prisoner of war in the United States."

At the Red Ox Inn in Heidelburg, the Americans were sitting at a long table and enjoying the rousing, beer-drinking atmosphere. "We were doing the *Student Prince* sort of thing, singing and swaying with steins of beer—having a great time," Al recalled. "Then someone started 'Meadowlands,' and we were la-la-ing the melody. In a moment, a tall German student came over, clicked his heels and said, 'I vish you vould not sing that Russian song.'"

Al had not realized the song was associated with Russia, but he stood up, banged the table and shouted, "Stop! We are Americans, and we do not sing that song!" The German students erupted in applause, and soon the Americans and their hosts had become a single bilingual party, which lasted far into the night.

In Berlin, members of the Glee Club were walking to their hotel at about 10 p.m. when they passed a bombed cathedral. They were examining the ruins when some of them climbed up onto piles of rubble and began to sing. Someone came out of a nearby tavern to investigate, and in a few minutes all the beer halls on the street emptied out to hear a Purdue Glee Club concert in the moonlight on the remains of a destroyed church. Wendell Swartz, who had served in the air war over Germany, surveyed the destruction around them and commented, "Boy I hope I didn't drop this one."

The six-week tour was a whirlwind of all-night train rides, days of sightseeing and meeting the local citizens, and evening concerts. By the evening of the last concert in Frankfurt, many of the singers were sick from drinking the unfamiliar water. Al had to ask for volunteers for solos on the program, and several singers fled to the restrooms during the show.

Still the trip was a great success, and it was crowned with a stop in Wales, where the Glee Club had its first contact with the Obernkirchen Children's Choir of Buckeburg, Germany. The pigtailed children, aged six to seventeen, and the young men from Purdue took to one another instantly. The choir had been organized by its director, Edith Moeller, and the manager, Erna Pielsticker, as an activity for the war orphans of their town. "They were called 'Angels in Pigtails,' and when those kids sang, we just stood in the wings crying openly. It was the most heavenly sound we'd ever heard," Al said.

He sought out Miss Moeller after the concert, and as they shared a drink in her tent, he told her, despite the fact that neither spoke the other's language, that he would like her to bring the children to the United States. She was delighted by the prospect, and the Obernkirchen children eventually would capture hearts throughout America, with tours and television appearances.

Language was not a problem for the children and the Glee Clubbers either. After getting to know one another, the singers began to share music, and in a little while both groups appeared at Miss Moeller's tent to serenade their directors. The children sang, "Oh geeve me a hoom where ze boofalo roam," and the Glee Club sang "The Happy Wanderer." The rousing song had been written by Miss Moeller's brother, and it was destined to become an international standard, as well as a Purdue Glee Club favorite. In a corner of Al Stewart's living room stands a large doll wearing handmade traditional German clothes. He called this gift from the German children the most prized memento of his career.

"Of all the things I did and the people I met, I treasure the friendship we created between our boys and those children the most," he said. "That was the most rewarding experience I've ever had."

Although she didn't charm him quite as much as the Obernkirchen children, Queen Elizabeth II also made a favorable impression on Al when he met her during that first European trip. Theirs was a silent, ceremonial meeting, but the queen curtsied elaborately in recognition of the United States, and Al, who had been cynical about the pomp surrounding the queen, "faded right away. I never said a word to her, but she took me in 100 percent. I was sold on royalty from that minute, and if you asked me who the most charming woman I ever met was, I'd have to say Queen Elizabeth."

The Purdue Musical Organizations rode high in the 1950s and 1960s. Undoubtedly he could have coasted successfully for an indefinite time, but like all born leaders, Al constantly sought change and improvement. He kept a conservative hand on the musical styles of the groups, but he refined his organization and searched for new audiences. That first trip to Europe proved to be only a door opener. Other visits followed, and foreign travel came to be an expected part of the P.M.O. experience.

Fall tryouts for the Glee Club assumed mob proportions, as more and more students sought to be part of the most prestigious student group on campus. "Fraternities and residence halls would tell their new members whenever we'd announce the call-out—'Go over and try out for the Glee Club. You might get lucky.' We'd get a thousand trying out sometimes." To control the size of the call-outs, Al organized a system of auditioning students during their Day-on-Campus visits the summer before their freshman year. Students who indicated musical experience or interest on their university application forms were invited to audition during their visits. For some, these tryouts became lifetime memories. Al had long ago overcome the chore of repeating the same instructions to every candidate. The group got a terse, tape-recorded lecture on the rigors ahead for those who made the grade. Al had taped his spiel, so that he could sit in intimidating silence at the end of the long, narrow room. Students could sing any song they wanted in any key. Pianists like Bill Luhman and John Farley would accompany and were seldom stumped by a request. "I didn't make it easy on anybody," Al admitted. "I wasn't trying to be mean to the kids, but I was as much interested in how they handled themselves as I was in their voices. I couldn't afford to have a kid who was great in practice but would fall apart on stage."

As soon as the audition was over, the student was whisked through the door, measured for clothing and sent on his way. Those who made the Glee

All eyes in this photo, taken in the mid-1950s, appear to be focused on the same thing. Could it be Al Stewart?

Glee Clubbers and Purduettes harmonize at an After Glow party, following the 1960 meeting of the Indiana Society of Chicago.

Elaborately costumed musicals like this one combined resources and talents of P.M.O. and Purdue theater members in the late 1940s and the 1950s.

Club were sent a musical package with a Glee Club recording, a selection of music and instructions to report the week before classes for Glee Club summer camp. The camp is a kind of musical boot camp, held in a spartan atmosphere designed to turn confused freshmen into performers who will acquit themselves like professionals in front of an audience.

Under Al Stewart and subsequently under Bill Luhman and Bill Allen, the Glee Club camp was designed as an intense experience, but it was not anything like an initiation or a hazing. "The freshmen are there to learn what being part of the Glee Club means," Al explained. "Some of them have to be taught to walk and talk and how to eat in public, because a few days after they leave there, they might be at a reception with the president, and maybe they've never been off the farm before. If anything, the older guys take extra trouble to help the freshmen."

In 1937, Al had accepted an appointment as the nation's first state extension chorus director, and in that capacity he had overseen the organization of county choruses all around the state. The choruses, although never as well organized or as intensely run as the West Lafayette Campus groups, are an excellent diversion and a way to spread the positive influence of music. In the 1950s, Al refined the concept and began to promote "industrial music" as a way of improving morale and—perhaps—profits in large corporations. He spoke and wrote widely on the topic to companies that were interested in setting up choruses, and he even accepted a part-time appointment to direct the employee chorus for the Marshall Field department stores in Chicago for nine years.

In his speeches and in his work, he continued to promote the concept that music is a basic human pleasure, enjoyed most by the people who are making it:

> I believe that what this world needs as much as anything else is more homemade music—people around a piano or singing with a guitar or just singing in church. People can enjoy themselves so much if they just let the music take over their emotions. And they can be pretty good, too. I've always felt that a good director can get good music out of just about any group that's willing to do what he says.

> My favorite story on that is the one-penny story. If I could get everybody in the country to send me a penny—just one penny—no one would miss the penny, and I'd be rich as hell. But I'm just not a good enough organizer to get everybody to send their penny. I am a pretty good music director, though, and by getting everybody in the chorus to give just a little, I can make some pretty good music.

Al would prove points like that with various groups like the Indiana Home Demonstration Chorus, which assembles at Purdue once a year for meetings and one gigantic sing-along. In 1954, Al and Marvin Meyers took the 2,000-member chorus to California, where they sang in the Hollywood Bowl during a national convention.

Although he never had political aspirations or even sought the company of politicians, Al was a solid Republican, and through sheer exposure to great numbers of people, he made political connections which led to his being asked to serve as master of ceremonies at the party's national convention in 1956. During the lengthy convention proceedings, he and the orchestra leader began talking and lost track of where the program had progressed. Suddenly, they became aware of an uncharacteristic quiet, and they concluded that they had missed a cue. The orchestra was stopped just in time from striking up "There'll Be a Hot Time in the Old Town Tonight" during a moment of silence for a deceased party dignitary.

That sort of lapse was rare because the natural fear of appearing before an audience never existed for Al Stewart. "I've always been perfectly comfortable on stage," he claimed. "I don't know why, but I feel at home there." This state of relaxation freed him to improvise, change programs in mid-show and kid around with entertainers. Jeanne Smith (nee Jeanne St. Pierre), a member of the Choraleers in the mid-1950s, remembers how Al announced during a show for a convention of fertilizer manufacturers that she had accepted the fraternity pin of Glee Club member John Fisher. The romance was complicated by the fact that she had recently dated the Glee Club's manager, Rene Warnicke. To the assembled strangers, Al proclaimed them a "beautiful triangle" before releasing the embarrassed students. Far from resenting this, the three remember it fondly, says Jeanne, who ultimately married Neil Smith, another Glee Clubber. "Al always knew just how far he could go with an individual," she said.

The Smiths' lives and careers also were affected by their P.M.O. experiences. After Neil graduated in 1956, he joined the U.S. Army and received a Special Services assignment to the Army Chorus, where he replaced Steve Lawrence. This led to a career in broadcasting, and Neil and Jeanne now are members of a successful consulting firm in Washington.

Sheila Johnston Klinker also found her life changed by her musical experiences at Purdue. When she transferred from Butler University in 1958, Sheila Johnston already had sung professionally for several years, primarily with Art Flanagan, a band leader who had worked as an arranger for Glenn Miller and Perry Como. She had toured most of the Midwest and had performed with Ella Fitzgerald, the Andrews Sisters and Jerry Lee Lewis. She had an offer from Flanagan to join him on his next tour. Despite her experience and success, Klinker was intimidated when she auditioned for Al Stewart, and characteristically he didn't let on that he was impressed. "He said he thought he might find a place for me," she recounts.

But she was better than the usual run of college girl singers, and, of course, Al knew it. The next day, he sent word for her to show up at the Glee Club's first-nighter show, and she soloed that night. From then on, she was a soloist with the Purduettes, and she worked regularly in professional engagements Al booked for her. Still, she remained "scared to death" of the director throughout her student career. One day, while in class, she received a message to report to Al. He told her she had an immediate appointment to see Cecelia Zissis, dean of women, to interview for the Miss Purdue contest.

"I said, 'Al, that's a *beauty* contest! I'm too fat.' But he just insisted, said don't worry about anything. So I went over there wearing these old clothes and tennis shoes and feeling like a fool. That night, Dean Zissis called and said I was it. I was Miss Purdue in the Miss Indiana Contest. Can you imagine?"

Billed as "Miss Music of Purdue," Klinker wound up as second runner-up in the contest held in Michigan City. The pageant included a bathing suit competition, although Al had promised her it wouldn't.

"That was just his way of getting me through my hang-up up about the bathing suit," she says. "I just never would have done anything like that on my own, but you see, Al had a way of building people up, perhaps even exaggerating their talent, and they would rise to his expectations. He gave me the ability and the background that made me feel comfortable with people. I'm a very shy person who has spent her whole life speaking in front of groups of people, and it's because of Al that I can do that."

After graduating from Purdue in 1961, Klinker began a career teaching in the Lafayette school system, and in 1982, she was elected to the Indiana House of Representatives.

It could be argued that Al's approach to handling students was overly paternalistic and that he overstepped his authority by pressuring a student into an activity, but two things mitigate strongly in his favor. First of all, he seems always to have chosen wisely when he singled out a student for special attention, and the individuals emerged the better for it. Sheila Johnston Klinker's fond gratitude is a typical response. Second, Al's approach with his students was perfectly consistent with the way he handled his own life and career. Just as some people seem to be born without the fear of heights, Al Stewart had no fear of failure. Perhaps because he knew poverty so intimately as a boy and as a young man, it had lost its ability to intimidate him. England's Queen Elizabeth I once told her subjects that if she were cast out of her palace with nothing but a petticoat, she would rise again to a high state through her own resourcefulness. The same sort of confidence seems to have ruled Al Stewart's life. At Purdue, he had begun with nothing, and through a combination of ability, audacity and commitment that almost approached alchemy, he had built one of the finest musical organizations in the country. The process was difficult, but never tedious, and he had no reason to doubt that he could do it again.

In 1960, one of the great honors of Al's life came to him when DePauw University's Board of Trustees voted to award him an honorary doctoral degree in music. While he relished the recognition itself, it was especially satisfying because it allowed him to be referred to as Dr. Stewart, and this, in a small way, made up for the degree he had been forced to forgo nearly three decades earlier. The lack of money had forced him to miss out on schooling, but he hadn't missed out on the education, and that was the beauty of the DePauw degree. It didn't just honor his achievements, it recognized the *fact* that he was an authority in his field, an innovator, and a true force in music. Because of Al's success at Purdue, his profession had changed. Some programs modeled themselves after his; directors changed the way they worked because he had made them look at things in new ways.

He taught his singers a commonsense, easily understood approach to choral music that demanded a certain amount of discipline, but also allowed them room to express emotion and to enjoy the experience of singing. It is this enjoyment—this joy—coming through the music that produces the Purdue sound. When the music is at its best, the audience hears what seems to be a group of good friends singing for old times' sake—but singing far better than any group of friends ever manages to sing on its own.

Some of the secret is revealed in this explanation from Al:

> The human voice is a wind instrument. It is not a percussion instrument. That's where most people go wrong. You strike a piano or a guitar to produce music, but if you strike a flute, you get noise. So with the voice, you must use wind, and the wind is like gasoline is to a car. You might have a Mercedes or a Cadillac, but without gas, you won't go anywhere. And you may have the best voice in the world, but if you don't learn how to breathe, you aren't going to sing much.
>
> The letters that we call vowels are the only ones meant to produce continuous tones. The consonants are used at the beginning and the end of vowels to make words, and the result is language. When they sing, a lot of people make the mistake of holding the consonants, and that's when you get terrible-sounding groups, because they're all dragging out those consonants, and if everybody's singing an *s*, you get this terrible hissssssing sound. I try to teach the kids to attack that consonant, then leave it just as quickly. When we're singing about the Deity, it's "Gaawwd!" Draw out the vowel sound, stop on the consonants. Of course, then we have to get everybody to do it together.

Perhaps just as important as his teaching techniques were Al's unique programming methods. He always maintained that his greatest talent was his ability to "be the audience," to somehow sense the mood of the group before him and give the people the music they wanted to hear. Because of this, he directed concerts for more than forty years without using printed programs. This method meant that his singers had to be ready to produce on a moment's notice, any one of about one hundred fifty songs in their repertoire—a challenge for any group, but an even more formidable possibility for those who might be called on to sing a solo number at any time. This readiness to respond inspired awe in Fred Waring when he directed the Glee Club during a visit to Purdue.

After the group had followed his direction perfectly through several numbers, Waring said, "My singers could not do what you have just done. This is a remarkable organization."

Al's approach to a program was to give the audience a kind of vocal rollercoaster ride—several breathtaking experiences spaced around a series of lesser thrills, with the added dimension of contrasting emotions thrown in. Just as the great tragedians always provided comic relief to allow the audience to catch its breath, he varied the pace and the mood to accentuate experiences.

"An audience can only take so much," he explained. "If you give them all high drama, they won't be able to come up to it, and if you give them all novelty numbers they get tired of that. By mixing things up the right way, people can feel all the emotions more deeply, and they go away having heard just enough."

One of Al's favorite devices for explaining music was a statue of Michelangelo's David, which he kept along with a plain block of rectangular marble:

> I had seen the David many times in Florence, but it never meant that much to me, although it's a beautiful statue. But one time I took a tour, and a woman guide said that the David had been created from a single huge piece of marble—that's what Michelangelo had started with. Now you and I would just see the block of marble, but she said Michelangelo looked at it and saw within it this beautiful statue that the Lord had put there. And

In 1958, Edith Moeller, director of the Obernkirchen Children's Choir, and some of her singers presented this costumed doll to Al Stewart as a symbol of the friendship that developed between the Glee Club and the "Angels in Pigtails."

The ruins of Pompeii, outside Naples, Italy, were the scene of an impromptu concert in 1964.

Foreign travel became routine for the Glee Club in the 1950s. This picture was taken as the group departed for Europe in 1956.

The Scholars were a Glee Club act specializing in the folk music of the mid-1960s. In 1966, the group consisted of Jack Strite, Cal Yoke and John Le Leur.

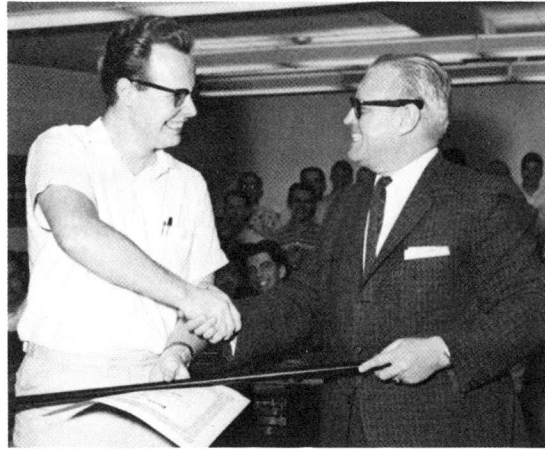

Although he was at Purdue for only a year, Holger Schmidt-Hamann sang his way into Al Stewart's Hall of Fame.

The generation gap was bridged at the 1983 Christmas Show. The trio at left is Chris Hunter, Kerri Klinker and Beth McDonald. At right are Sheila Klinker (Kerri's mother), Sonya Eddy (daughter of Al Stewart) and Marilyn Kingma.

A rare moment of relaxation at Glee Club camp in the early 1970s.

Industrial conference concerts, like this one in 1950, became a big part of the Glee Club's bookings in the postwar era.

what he did with his hammer and chisel was uncover it so the rest of us could see it, too.

When I heard that, I said, "By God! That's exactly what I've been trying to say about music for years." When a composer writes a piece of music, he has an idea in his mind of what it should sound like, and it's our job as musicians and singers to uncover that and let the rest of the world hear it. Right after that, I got me a little statue of the David and a piece of marble about the same size, and I use that to explain music to people.

Most of the young men who are the lifeblood of the Purdue Glee Club seem to come from small midwestern towns and farms. The singing group provides them not only a musical outlet, but a springboard to sophistication that they wouldn't acquire until much later, if at all, without the Purdue Musical Organizations' influence.

An exception to this pattern was Holger Schmidt-Hamann, a German boy who turned up in Al's office for a Glee Club audition in 1960. He walked in carrying a sheet of music, did not flinch under the spotlight aimed at him the length of the long, narrow room, and effortlessly sang in one of the finest voices Al had ever heard at Purdue. "You're pretty good," Al told him when he'd finished singing. "You have a lot of schmaltz—do you know what that is?"

"Ya, stomach," said Schmidt-Hamann.

"Close enough," Al replied.

Holger Schmidt-Hamann stayed at Purdue one year, during which he sang beautifully and became one of the hundreds of students who made Al and Charlotte's kitchen a second home. Al knew that a businessman from southern Indiana had sponsored Holger's entry into the country, but the boy seemed to need money, so the Stewarts paid him a dollar an hour to do odd jobs. He mowed grass, cleaned the garage, washed windows—whatever Al and Charlotte could think of that would make the money seem something other than a gift.

Schmidt-Hamann liked Purdue, and he liked the Stewarts, but he aspired to a professional singing career in his native country, and he left after one year. It was 1964 before Al saw him again. During a Glee Club trip to Europe, the phone in Al's Amsterdam hotel room rang, and a voice on the line said: "Holger Schmidt-Hamann here speaking."

Al and Mickey accepted an invitation to visit Schmidt-Hamann's home, which turned out to be less like a burgher's cottage than a baron's estate. The place featured servants, a ballroom, assorted limousines and a Steinway grand for the party which the host had planned for the Glee Club. The German boy Charlotte and Al had befriended had been the son of one of the largest auto-parts retailers in the world, and Holger now was running the family business.

As Al pieced the story together later, Schmidt-Hamann's father had sent him to Purdue as a compromise. The son had wanted to pursue a musical career, the father wanted him to study engineering. A business associate from Indiana had told them, "There's a university in my state where he can do both. Send him to Purdue, and tell him to see Al Stewart."

The Stewarts visited Schmidt-Hamann several times after that, and in the late 1970s Holger returned to West Lafayette, where he looked out the Stewarts' front window one morning and said, "I think I should have a house here." Al picked up the phone and called Manny Cibrian at Boardwalk Realty. "I've got a hot one here; you'd better come over," he told the Realtor.

Schmidt-Hamann bought a home near the Stewarts' residence in the Indian Trails section of West Lafayette. He filled it with furniture and a live-in caretaker—a friend of Al's who was a fraternity house cook. On his infrequent visits to Lafayette, Schmidt-Hamann stayed in the house. Otherwise, it simply was maintained for him.

Chapter 13

Shortly before his retirement from Purdue, Al Stewart still had the dynamic personality that had built P.M.O. into a world-renowned singing aggregate.

END OF AN ERA

The late 1960s and early 1970s brought sweeping changes to college campuses, and Al didn't like most of them. Although Purdue remained calm compared to some other Big Ten schools—and was called "a hotbed of rest" by a national magazine—political protests did erupt on campus in 1971, and the whole ambience changed. Hair was longer; students and faculty alike "dressed down" in tattered clothing and unkempt beards. A brief takeover of the union building was "disgusting" in Al's opinion. "That was a black day for Purdue. They did every low thing you can think of in there. They urinated on the floors and just generally acted like animals."

Although short, neat haircuts and well-tailored clothes were no longer fashionable for student leaders, styles did not change for the Glee Club or other P.M.O. groups. In fact, a renewed camaraderie and a fiercer kind of pride took over. Although membership in the Glee Club or the Purduettes didn't carry the universal status it had during the 1950s and early 1960s, the singers remained as committed as ever, and they made no apologies. "Our kids were smart enough to know that all those weirdos weren't worth worrying about," Al commented.

Bob Ford, a bass soloist from 1968 through 1972 who later became president of the P.M.O. Club, a fund-raising organization, remembers getting a secret thrill from the double takes people did when he walked across campus in full formal dress on the way to a concert:

> Sure you looked different, but I knew people were saying, "There go some Glee Club guys," and I was proud of that. We were special because we worked hard, and we were good.

> The group was always pro-university. There were some members who wanted to get involved physically against the demonstrators in those days, but I don't think that ever happened. We just weren't part of that scene.
>
> We had no longhairs. If you couldn't see the top of your ears or if you had a big wad at the back of your neck, Al or Mickey sent you to the barbershop. That was part of the rules of the group. Either you conformed or you got out of the group. As far as I'm concerned, that's fair. It's a small price to pay to have your hair cut to be able to travel to Chicago, Atlanta, Miami, and Europe. Heck, we went to Hawaii my freshman year.

But Ford believes the travel and the glamor are only a small part of the Glee Club's appeal:

> Most of the guys who had to drop—if they had a grade problem, for instance—weren't worried about getting back in because they wanted to go to Europe. They wanted to get back in so they could be part of the group, to be involved in the fellowship, to sing. Anybody who hasn't done it can't imagine what it's like to stand up there and just get an audience in the palm of your hand—to make them feel what you want them to feel.
>
> We took it as a challenge when somebody in the audience acted uninterested or bored. We'd think, "I'm going to get that guy!" and we'd try to throw everything right at him until he was feeling the thrill. When you've done that with someone, you've really accomplished something.

Ford, who became the general manager of WLFI-TV in Lafayette and became known as the color man for telecasts of Purdue basketball games, was one of the busiest students in Purdue's history. During the four years he was a Glee Club soloist, he also was a star of the varsity basketball team, ending up as the twelfth leading career scorer in Boilermaker history. Coming out of Evansville North High School, Ford was the most heavily recruited basketball player in the state, and his final choice was between Indiana University and Purdue. He made it clear that he wanted to sing, as well as play basketball, and both schools recruited him on that basis.

"The difference was that at Indiana, they told me I was in whether I could sing or not. At Purdue, Al said, 'If you can sing, then you can be in the group.

Al met President Richard Nixon at the Hilton Hotel in Washington, D.C., in 1974.

Charlotte and Al got into the spirit of the Islands for this photo, taken during a Glee Club visit to Hawaii.

Purdue President Arthur G. Hansen was a devoted fan of the Glee Club and Al Stewart. This commencement performance took place during Al's last year as P.M.O. director.

If you can't sing, you won't be in the group.' I liked that better than a free gift, and I chose Purdue."

So Purdue's Varsity Glee Club may have the distinction of being the only singing group that can take credit for improving its school's basketball record.

Kenneth Knowles, a Glee Club contemporary of Ford's and now a professional singer in Indianapolis, finds that he still draws on his P.M.O. repertoire as well as on the social graces he learned through the Glee Club. "I was a farm boy from Covington, Indiana, and I just learned a tremendous amount very fast," he says. "We mingled with many different kinds of people, and I learned to be comfortable with them all. I also learned to be a pro about being ready to sing when I had to. You don't always go on exactly on time, but Al didn't have any use of prima donnas."

Knowles, who later studied operatic techniques, found that in the Glee Club he had "almost overlearned" such basics as diaphragm breathing. "The great lesson I learned," he says, "is watch the director. I could focus on Al and just screen everything else out. We all learned that. Once, during a performance, he kept rubbing his jaw, and we were all going crazy, trying to figure out what it meant. It turned out he'd been to the dentist, and the Novocain was wearing off."

Al Stewart entered the 1970s, knowing that retirement was not far ahead. The university's mandatory-retirement policy would require that he step down in 1974, although he had suffered no loss of vigor and was still refining the musical organizations. In 1970 he hired Bill Allen as an assistant director because Allen combined a love of choral music with a strong formal education in music theory. Al believed Allen would strengthen the organization and that he was a potential director.

In 1972 Al streamlined the University Choir, ending the practice of leaving the choir open to anyone who wanted to sing. The choir had grown to more than three hundred voices, most of them female. To balance the group, its size was limited to sixty-six voices. To accommodate some of the singers who were screened out of the choir, an all-female Choral Club was formed under Bill Luhman's direction, but this group was limited to about seventy places, filled by auditions.

Although he suffered from a painful arthritic condition in his knees, Al's general health remained excellent, and he approached retirement reluctantly; but as the end of his Purdue era approached, a tide of recognition began to build. He had been named an honorary alumnus of Purdue in 1972, but the most meaningful tributes were much less formal. They came in the form of nearly six thousand people who crowded the Elliott Hall of Music for his last concert on March 22, 1974. They came in the form of more than three hundred former Glee Club members from half the states in the Union, who gathered on stage to prove what one of them claimed thirty years after graduation: "If we found ourselves standing in front of Al on the podium after all these years, we'd instinctively hit the right notes when he gave the downbeat." And they came in the form of letters, thousands of them—enough to fill three bulging volumes. They were neatly typed on expensive watermarked stationery, and they were scribbled hastily on notebook paper. They came from senators, and company presidents and from show business celebrities; but mostly they came from the people who sang for Al Stewart and who are his monument.

The letters said things like: "When I became a part of the P.M.O. Choir, I discovered the real joy of singing my heart out." And: "You have brought sunshine to my life." And: "You will never know the joy you have given..."

And one asked a single question: "How do you retire an institution?"

Chapter 14

As director of P.M.O., Bill Luhman wanted to remain faithful to the Al Stewart tradition, but he added some innovations of his own.

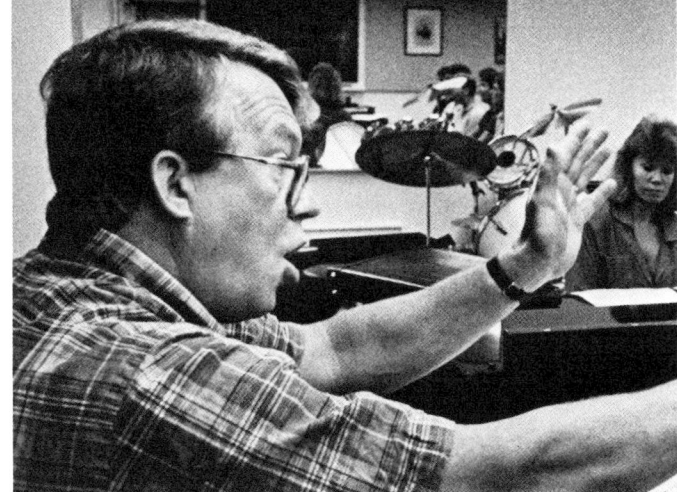

Directing a rehearsal at the Elliott Hall of Music in 1986, Bill Allen shows the dynamic quality that marks the Glee Club's performances under his leadership. The accompanist is Diane Thompson.

LUHMAN AND ALLEN: ON WITH THE SHOW!

Al Stewart's recommendation on his retirement was that Mickey McGuire and Bill Luhman be named co-directors of P.M.O. He had discussed the directorship with both of them, but neither had been eager to take the job. Al believed that either could be successful and that the co-directorship would encourage one of them to emerge as the likely choice. Shared appointments are not common at Purdue, however, and upon Al's retirement, Bill Luhman was named acting director of P.M.O. by William Fischang, vice president for student services. A year later, the Luhman appointment was made permanent.

Bill Luhman was perhaps the most remarkable musician ever to be associated with Purdue. Al Stewart described him as "the only person I ever met with absolutely perfect pitch. If you said C sharp to him, he would sing C sharp, and if C sharp on your piano didn't sound the same, there was something wrong with your piano." It was with the piano that Luhman first impressed Al. After coming to Purdue from Fort Wayne as a seventeen-year-old freshman in 1943, he amazed people on campus with his piano wizardry in informal get-togethers at the union and other hangouts. Word spread to Al Stewart that "you have to hear this freshman play the piano," and after listening to one number, Al knew he had found a valuable commodity. Luhman became P.M.O.'s first paid accompanist. He played the piano for all the singing groups, and, as an economics major with a good head for figures, helped with the P.M.O. books.

The value of Luhman as an accompanist was explained by Bob Ford, who sang with him years later:

> You could sit down on the keyboard and he could tell you the width of your rear end by which keys were at either end. He could play anything in any key at any time. He would change things around in your solo. If he thought you were loafing, he'd take it up a half step. If he thought you had a cold, he'd take it down a step, so you didn't have to crack on the top notes.
>
> I was fairly famous for changing keys in the middle of a song. It didn't bother Bill. He'd change with me. He made you sound good whether you were good or not. He was always there. If the group was having a problem, if the baritones were having trouble hearing their part, all of a sudden, in the accompaniment, the baritone part stuck out until they got back on track.
>
> He knew so much. There was so much talent inside his head and inside his hands. The entertainment for us at camp would just be Bill giving a concert on the piano. He could play anything from the dirtiest, rottenest novelty number ever written, up to the most difficult Bach piece. It's hard to put into words what he meant to the group. He was a great musician, and a great friend to the kids.

Ford was talking about the mature Luhman of the early 1970s. Bill Luhman the student had so much fun working for the musical organizations that he took his time getting through college. He carried light credit loads so that he could devote more time to his musical avocation, and he didn't receive his bachelor of science degree until 1949.

After graduation, Luhman took a job as an assistant credit manager with Fisher Paper Company in Fort Wayne. Two years later, he became an accountant for Fruehauf Trailer Company, also in his hometown. In 1954, he took another accounting job, this one including the title of Fort Wayne's office manager, for Fort Wayne's O'Reilly Office Supply Company. In 1957, he returned to Purdue to work for Al Stewart with the title assistant to the director of the Purdue Musical Organizations. Later he would get a promotion to associate director.

Luhman's presence on the staff meant that Al had a fantastic accompanist who also was a fine arranger and a man absolutely loyal to P.M.O. The combination of Stewart, the driving genius; McGuire, the dynamic executive officer; and Luhman, the inspired musician, helped bring P.M.O. into full flower.

The organization which Bill Luhman inherited from Al Stewart was a healthy and growing one. Artistically, the Glee Club was perhaps the best men's amateur choral group in the country; financially, P.M.O. had prospered through its prestigious bookings and through private donations to the P.M.O. Club, which had developed a sophisticated fund-raising operation. Besides paying travel expenses, P.M.O. was able to underwrite the onstage clothing requirements of members and to provide scholarships in some cases.

Although he was devoted to the vision of P.M.O. he had absorbed from Al during more than twenty years of association, Luhman put his personal stamp on the organization. Where Al ruled through the force of his personality and, when necessary, through fear, Luhman developed friendly relationships with his singers. Bill Allen, who worked under both directors, said, "The kids loved Bill Luhman; they would have walked through fire for him. Bill didn't do things the way Al did because he wasn't Al, but he got respect by his example and because of the kind of musician he was."

As director, Luhman wanted to retain the excellence and the reputation of the Glee Club and the Purduettes, but he also wanted to improve the status of the other P.M.O. units. The streamlining of the University Choir and the formation of the Choral Club in 1972 had given him two groups of manageable size for public performances, and he felt that both would improve if given more opportunities to perform. Under Luhman's directorship, two eighteen-member English hand-bell choirs were created by Dennis Yount, an assistant director. The all-female Purdue Belles and the Purdue Mixed-Bell Choir were an instant success on Christmas Show programs and, surprisingly, more than eighty students came to the first call-out for the groups.

"Bill believed the groups that had taken a back seat to the Glee Club and Purduettes would be more fun for the students and better musically if given a reason to exist, and the best reason is performing," Allen said. "That doesn't mean he was going to downplay the Glee Club. He just felt there was plenty of opportunity for all of them, and he worked to take advantage of that."

The Glee Club indeed continued to thrive under Luhman, although some things changed. He increased the practice of using the Glee Club to sing background for soloists, and he encouraged the development of specialty singing groups within the Glee Club. Al had used such groups, too, including a barbershop quartet and a folk-singing group called the Raucous Trio, but Luhman made the specialty acts a larger part of his programs. In 1978, Ba-na-na, a rock-and-roll oldies group, was established with Dave Klimes, Mike Hummerickhouse, Chris Kirk and Kenny Beals as the original members. A year later, the country-oriented Poison Oaks were formed with Jim Peterson, Doug Shelton, Jeff Cherry and Tom Loepker.

Luhman had only begun to make his mark on P.M.O. when tragedy struck. He was diagnosed as suffering from cancer in 1979. Treatment produced a partial remission which lasted for more than two years. He was able to take the Glee Club to Washington for the Reagan inauguration in 1981, but in August of 1982 the cancer was found to be spreading very rapidly once more. Still, Luhman continued to work until the night of the P.M.O. Club's Octoberfest that year. That night, Luhman was playing piano while Al Stewart directed alumni members of the Glee Club—the two old friends working together just as they had for so many years—when the physical effort of playing broke a bone in Luhman's weakened right arm. In a final valiant performance, he somehow finished the show, but he entered St. Elizabeth Hospital the next morning and died there on November 5, 1982. He was fifty-six.

Bill Allen directed the Purdue Glee Club for the first time just four days after Bill Luhman's death. He had become acting P.M.O. director immediately and would receive the permanent appointment as director in less than two weeks.

A native of Washington, Indiana, Allen has an extensive formal education and experience in music. He earned bachelor's degrees in music and in music education from the University of Cincinnati. After working as a supervisor of vocal music in an Ohio public school, he returned to the University of Cincinnati for a master's degree in choral music and piano, then stayed on as assistant to the dean of the university's College Conservatory of Music.

When Al Stewart hired him in 1970, Allen found that Purdue had a style of its own when it came to music. "In music school, we played head music," he explains. "Here we do heart music."

An accomplished pianist and organist, as well as a skilled director, Allen found that his extensive formal background in music could be an asset at Purdue, but that he had to adapt it to a new kind of environment:

> I was used to a very serious situation where everyone was thinking about careers in music, but these kids were doing it because they love it. They weren't getting any academic credit for their music, and they were proud of that, and I'm proud of it, too. There's a magic that comes from performing just for the love of it, and I think that's what Al Stewart gave us. He believed music had to be fun to be good, and that was the most valuable thing he taught me.

Allen's first big problem as director of P.M.O. was rebuilding the staff. The organization hadn't been at full strength since Al's retirement, because Bill Luhman had moved up and hadn't been replaced. The subsequent retirement of Mickey McGuire and then Luhman's death had offset the hiring of Dennis Yount and Diane Thompson as assistant directors in 1979. Allen added Jae Israel to his staff in 1983 and Gary Branson in 1985 to round out a team that is musically sound and young enough to build for the future.

"One of our strengths now is the age of the staff, which ranges from twenty-eight to forty-five," Allen says. "Everybody here now is sound musically and experienced in education, and they believe in the P.M.O philosophy. We can get better and better, and that's what we want."

Allen's vision of P.M.O.'s future is to maintain an emphasis on middle-of-the-road music, yet constantly keep up with current trends. "We're always going to do the war horses—the songs the alums want to do when they come back," he says, "but we want to adapt them to our style and stay up to date.

The inset of this 1970 photo shows Bill Luhman, then the accompanist for the Glee Club.

Bill Luhman, as he looked shortly before his graduation from Purdue in 1949. A gifted pianist, Luhman performed as a P.M.O. accompanist throughout his student years.

Ba-Na-Na, a specialty group which sings revived 1950s rock-and-roll music, has become a popular Glee Club act. The 1984 version of the group consisted of Chuck Nalon, Mark Erwin, Tony Avellana and Roger Winstead.

Handbell choirs became popular with both audiences and student musicians after two eighteen-member groups were established under Bill Luhman's directorship of P.M.O. This photo shows both the all-female Purdue Belles and the Purdue Mixed-Bell Choir.

Bill Luhman and the Glee Club were at center stage for Ronald Reagan's inauguration as president in 1981.

Bill Allen is intent on his music during a rehearsal at the Glee Club camp at Rose-Hulman Institute of Technology in 1975. Allen is an accomplished pianist and organist, as well as a director.

This group of Glee Clubbers entertained at a 1977 Kick-Off Coffee at a home in West Lafayette.

And we will never use a published arrangement of a song. Everything we sing is arranged by a member of the staff."

Allen credits Diane Thompson with adding to P.M.O.'s repertoire by constantly searching out and arranging new material. Thompson, the first woman to accompany the Glee Club on piano, studied voice at Indiana University and has a background that includes work as a supper club singer and pianist. She also has worked with Dennis Yount to modernize the image of the Purduettes, which Yount directs.

Yount has changed the Purduettes' musical emphasis from old standards to contemporary music and show tunes; has added choreography to their shows, along with bass and drum accompaniment; and has had their costumes redesigned. A music graduate of Butler University, Yount found Purdue's approach to music "unique."

"It's hard for a musical purist to adjust," he says. "The book is thrown away. Music school teaches you that a quarter note is a quarter note, but that's not always true here. Things are very dynamic, but it works."

Under Jae Israel's leadership, extension music has begun to grow again in Indiana. When she joined P.M.O. in 1983, she began trying to recruit younger singers for the county choruses, and has managed to lower the average age from sixty to forty-five. At the same time, Israel, formerly choral director at McCutcheon High School, has increased participation to about one thousand members—an increase of about three hundred. With about fifty counties organized, she believes the extension choruses may bounce back even further.

With a staff that is eager and creative, Allen believes he has the tools to bring P.M.O. into the next century stronger than ever:

> We are in very good shape today. Part of that is the staff, but part of it is the students, too. I am just amazed when these kids go out and mix with alumni and trustees and administrators. We can go to Florida or California and they just bring the campus with them. It makes those people feel like they're back here at Purdue again.
>
> Students today are more free to express themselves than they've ever been, and our kids have chosen to express themselves in a positive way.

Musically, it's wonderful because they can do things that astonish me. They don't know enough to be intimidated by difficult music. They just do it.

People who have sung under Allen or during the Allen-Luhman transition support Allen's claim that P.M.O.'s strength and vitality continue to grow, but they tend to share the credit with their directors. Sandra Parker Owens, who sang for Allen in the University Choir from 1972 through 1976, believes that "no collegiate group represents the best ideals of young people today like P.M.O. My four years with the choir was one of the happiest, most rewarding experiences of my life. I think one of the unique things about it—and I know this is still true—is that when you fell below what you knew were P.M.O. standards, you really felt bad. No one had to tell you. There is just great pride."

Although she hadn't known a choir existed when she came to Purdue from Columbus, Indiana, Owens auditioned because she liked the mixed-voice sound of the group. With Allen's encouragement, she formed a successful trio with Sally Grigsby Vaught and Susan Bailey Elliott. "I never would have done that on my own," she says, "but Bill made us believe in ourselves. He was wonderful with the choir because of the personal attention he gave everyone. We were trying to build the choir's reputation then, and we really needed that."

Pamela Wendt Whitcomb and her husband, Steve, met—and eventually married—through their Glee Club/Purduettes experience. Graduating in the mid-1970s, they developed a strong respect for all three of P.M.O's directors and for the training they received at the university with no music school. Both have sung with the Houston Symphony Chorale, and Mrs. Whitcomb says, "It just amazes people that we've had no formal training." Mrs. Whitcomb remembers running across the Purdue campus from Elliott Hall to her room in McCutcheon Hall "so I could call my parents and tell them I made the Purduettes." She calls her P.M.O. days "a precious experience." Allen, she says, is an outstanding director. "He interprets music so well, and he understands how to get the most from a group."

Getting maximum performance from people who are singing for fun, rather than for any hope of reward, has been the key to the success of choral music at Purdue. Somehow, the quality of the singing has been refined and nourished to world-class quality, while that fragile sense of fun has been preserved and even enhanced. It began in the heart of Al Stewart; it continued during the brief leadership of Bill Luhman; and today Bill Allen carries it on and searches for new and ever more challenging horizons. He knows better than anyone else how difficult the job is, but he says there is joy in meeting the challenge:

> We can never stand still, because this is a creative environment. We have bright young people who want to do things that haven't been done before, and I feel the same way. But we also have to hang onto the wonderful tradition that Al Stewart created and Bill Luhman preserved. The music must change and grow—not rapidly, but continually—but the ideals of P.M.O. will not change. I want the alumni of twenty years from now to say the same things I'm hearing alumni saying today.

Afterword

Having been a small part of Purdue Musical Organizations for sixteen of its fifty-six years, I join with thousands of P.M.O. alumni and friends who look upon this organization as special—and after reading this great book—even incredible.

This book is a tribute to the men and women who have left their marks at this great university through P.M.O. It is to Al and Charlotte Stewart, Mickey McGuire, Bill Luhman, Theo and Helen Agnew, Marvin and Grace Meyers, Rosemary Funk, and countless other dedicated staff members for their love and devotion.

I feel a part of something very special indeed. But now we look to the future—to Dennis Yount, Diane Thompson, Gary Branson, and Jae Israel, to the Glee Club, Purduettes, University Choir, and Handbell Choirs, to Extension Homemakers Chorus and State 4-H Chorus. P.M.O.'s philosophy of No Fun without Music and No Music without Fun will be paramount and will guide us as we move into the twenty-first century. We will continue to grow and develop new groups and traditions, but the underlying philosophy will always remain the same: Wholesome family entertainment by clean-cut, dedicated, attractive young men and women with a song in their hearts and love of their God, country, and university.

William E. Allen

P.M.O. Photo Gallery
A Representative Selection of Photos from the P.M.O. Archives

University Choir, 1975.

University Choir, 1980.

Choral Club, 1975, at the Purdue Memorial Union.

The 1980 Choral Club on the Elliott Hall of Music stage.

The Varsity Glee Club, 1945.

Glee Clubs of the late 1940s were beginning to include some older faces as war veterans returned home and enrolled at Purdue.

The Glee Club in 1955.

The 1960–61 Glee Club.

The Glee Club in 1965.

The Glee Club, 1975.

The Glee Club, 1980.

171

The 1986 Varsity Glee Club.

Appendix A. *P.M.O. Hall of Fame Members*

The Al Stewart Hall of Fame

Richard Thornton, 1941, Elkhart, Indiana*
Marvin Smith, 1942, Lafayette
David Simpson, 1943, Homewood, Illinois
William Kennedy, 1947, Shelbyville
William E. Luhman, 1949, Fort Wayne
Bruce "Mickey" McGuire, 1949, Seymour
J. Peter Smith, 1949, Indianapolis
Robert J. Tam, 1951, Burnettsville
Darrel Eubank, 1951, Louisville, Kentucky
John M. High, 1952, Kokomo
William McCain, 1953, Brookston
C. William Bugh, 1953, Brookston
Frank O'Brien, 1954, Lafayette
Alfred Hemmer, 1958, Dale
Joseph Cave, 1958, Greenfield
Isaac Peltnovich, 1958, Colon, Panama
Gary Jackson, 1959, North Manchester
James McKeand, 1960, Shelbyville
Holger Schmidt-Hamann, 1961, Hamburg, Germany
C. David Cochard, 1962, Greenfield
Larry Hausenfluck, 1963, Cutler
James C. Porter, 1964, Reisterstown, Maryland
Larry E. Russell, 1965, Sullivan
David L. Horne, 1966, Richmond
James F. Lattes, 1966, Lafayette
James A. Griffiths, 1966, Oxford
Russell Jay Wunderlich, 1967, Joliet, Illinois
Richard O. Plothaw, 1969, Bunker Hill
Mack Shultz, 1970, Montpelier
Kenneth H. Knowles, 1971, Veedersburg
Michael W. Chung, 1971, Mishawaka
Robert A. Ford, 1972, Evansville
David L. Pope, 1972, Munster
David R. Stith, 1973, Columbus
Leonard P. Pohlar, 1973, Batesville
Willie L. Standifer, 1973, Gary
Phillip A. Ballard, 1973, Marion
Keith A. Tonne, 1974, West Lafayette
Michael J. Middleton, 1975, Monticello
Donald Lee, 1976, Connersville
Stephen Whitcomb, 1976, Bunker Hill
Mark S. Loepker, 1977, Lafayette

*Unless otherwise specified, cities and towns in this list are located in Indiana.

The Bill Luhman Hall of Fame

Michael Needham, 1979, Mishawaka
John Myers, 1979, Marion
Jeff Cherry, 1981, Lafayette
James A. Hubert, 1981, West Lafayette
Doug Shelton, 1981, Lafayette

The Bill Allen Hall of Fame

Robert W. Martin,* 1983, Lafayette
Donald J. King,* 1983, Lafayette
Brian S. Dean,* 1983, Speedway
Bryan W. Lane, 1983, Lafayette
Christopher N. Shelton, 1984, Lafayette
Charles W. Nalon,** 1986, Glens Falls, New York
Brian T. Koning, 1986, West Lafayette

* Raucous Trio
** Ba-Na-Na

Appendix B. *A Hall of Music Who's Who*

Selected Entertainers Who Have Appeared in the Elliott Hall of Music

1943
October 23: Milt Britton, Bonnie Baker
November 23: The Vagabonds, Art Kassel

1944
September 1: George Olsen and Orchestra
October 6: Les Brown and Orchestra
November 17: Earl Carroll's Vanities

1945
January 2: Eddy Howard and Orchestra
April 6: Frankie Masters and Orchestra
June 8: Lawrence Welk and Orchestra
November 16: Eddie Oliver
November 21: Charlie Spivak

1946
January 6: Glenn Gray
January 8: Tommy Dorsey
March 29: Bobby Sherwood
April 6: Tex Benecke
July 12: Alvino Rey
August 15: Claude Thornhill
September 27: Fred Waring
November 1: Xavier Cugat
November 22: Woody Herman

1947
March 22: Fred Waring
March 28–29: Spike Jones
April 26: Raymond Scott
May 13: Gene Krupa
June 18: Frankie Masters
October 24: Fred Waring

October 25: Spike Jones
October 31: Wayne King
November 15: Danny Kaye
November 21: Jerry Colonna, Bob Burns

1949
January 16: Stan Kenton
March 9–10: Bob Hope
March 18–19: *High Button Shoes*
May 15: Vaughn Monroe
May 28: Horace Heidt
June 23: Lawrence Welk and Orchestra
July 7: *Showboat*
September 31–October 1: *Oklahoma!*
October 8–9: Hoagy Carmichael
October 21–22: Jo Stafford, Frank Sinatra, Tommy Dorsey
October 25–26: *Brigadoon*
November 20: Carmen Cavallaro, Tito Guizar
November 30: Fred Waring
December 2: Eddie Cantor

1950
January 27–28: *Icelandia*
February 28: The Wayne King Show
October 27–28: Elliott Lawrence, Benny Goodman
November 11: Ralph Flanagan
November 25: Frankie Carle

1951
February 24: Morton Downey
March 9–10: Spike Jones

October 13: *Don Juan in Hell* (with Charles Laughton, Agnes Moorehead, Sir Cedric Hardwicke and Charles Boyer)
November 17: Duke Ellington, Sarah Vaughan, Nat King Cole

1952
February 2: The Barbershop Revue
March 14: Spike Jones

1953
October 17: The Sauter-Finegan Orchestra
October 24: Bob Hope
November 20: Fred Waring
November 28: The Percy Faith Orchestra, Tony Bennett

1954
October 9: Billy May's Orchestra
October 20: Fred Waring
November 12–13: Ed Sullivan, "Toast of the Town"

1955
October 18: Edgar Bergen
October 22: Patti Page
November 5: Ed Sullivan
November 12: Eddy Howard
November 20: The Mercury Caravan

1956
February 4: Bob Scobey Frisco Band
May 5: Harry Belafonte
September 24: Les Elgart
October 27: Russ Carlyle and Orchestra
November 3: Tony Martin, Tex Benecke
November 24: Fred Waring

1957
March 16: Louis Armstrong
September 28: Bob Hope
October 12: Eydie Gorme
October 26: The Ted Heath Show
November 16: Herb Shriner, Margaret Whiting
November 19: The Glenn Miller Orchestra

1958
April 17: Tommy Dorsey
October 18: Lou Breese
November 1: Benny Goodman
November 22: Fred Waring

1959
October 3: Bob Hope
October 10: Stan Kenton
October 24: Fred Waring
November 4: Jimmie Rodgers

1960
September 24: The Ralph Marterie Show
October 14–15: Shelley Berman
October 28–29: George Gobel
November 5: Pops Americana, Herb Shriner
November 19: Rosemary Clooney

1961
October 6–7: Carol Channing, Frankie Laine
October 12–14: Johnny Mathis
October 27–28: The Dancing Waters, Gene Sheldon
November 3–4: Carmel Quinn, The Art Van Damme Quintet
November 10–11: Count Basie, Charlie Weaver

1962
October 12–13: Bob Newhart
October 19–20: Gordon MacRae
November 2–3: Fred Waring

November 24: Connie Stevens

1963
January 8: The Kingston Trio
October 4–5: Peter, Paul, and Mary
October 25–26: The Brothers Four
November 8–9: Peter Nero
November 15–16: Nat King Cole

1964
February 12: Fred Waring
April 17–18: Earl Grant
September 25–26: Julie London
October 9–10: Jimmy Dean
October 30–31: Senor Wences
November 20–21: The Ford Caravan

1965
September 17–18: Alan Sherman
September 24–25: Bobby Vinton
October 22–23: John Gary, The Osmond Brothers
November 5–6: Eydie Gorme, The Lettermen
November 12–13: Trini Lopez

1966
May 14: Count Basie, Peter Nero, Petula Clark
September 16–17: Louis Armstrong
September 30–October 1: The Smothers Brothers
October 7–8: John Davidson, Woody Herman
October 28–29: Roger Williams, Lainie Kazan
November 18–19: Robert Goulet

1967
April 29: The Baja Marimba Band, Nancy Wilson
September 29–30: Simon and Garfunkel
October 6–7: Mike Douglas
October 20–21: Henry Mancini
November 10–11: Ray Charles
November 17–18: Jack Benny

1968
May 18: The Al Hirt Variety Show
September 26–27: Sergio Mendes, The Kane Triplets
October 10–11: Gary Puckett and the Union Gap, The Baja Marimba Band
October 17–18: Dionne Warwick
October 24: Mantovani, Cliff Guest

1969
January 7–8: Jose Feliciano and Jose Greco

1970
March 7: The Fifth Dimension
May 10: Jonathan Winters, John Gary

1971
October 8–9: Sandler and Young, Peter Nero
October 30: Henry Mancini

1972
January 18: The Allman Brothers Band, The Ramsey Lewis Trio, Sonny and Cher
October 7: The Temptations
October 21: Henry Mancini
November 4: The Fifth Dimension
November 11: The Carpenters
November 29: The Beach Boys

1973
February 7: Gordon Lightfoot
April 6: Isaac Hayes
October 20: Anita Bryant, Pete Fountain
October 27: Doc Severinsen

November 14: John Denver

1974
October 12: Sandler and Young
November 2: Dionne Warwick

1976
October 16: Bill Cosby
October 22: Henry Mancini

1977
October 1: Gabe Kaplan
October 22: Henry Mancini

1978
September 23: Rich Little, Buddy Rich
November 4: The Captain and Tennille

1979
September 29: Doc Severinsen
October 27: Victor Borge

1980
October 4: Count Basie, Nancy Wilson
October 10: Bill Cosby, The Harmonicats
November 7: Lionel Hampton

1981
February 7: The Oak Ridge Boys

September 12: Larry Gatlin
September 26: The Manhattan Transfer, Martin Mull
October 10: Ella Fitzgerald
October 24: Red Skelton

1982
October 16: Henry Mancini

1983
September 10: Anne Murray
October 22: Bernadette Peters
October 29: Barbara Mandrell

1984
February 23: George Carlin
September 15: Ronnie Milsap, Sylvia
September 22: Liberace
October 13: George Burns
October 20: Amy Grant

1985
March 29: The Oak Ridge Boys
April 13: Eddie Murphy
July 6: Barry Manilow
October 13: The Beach Boys
October 26: Red Skelton
November 2: David Copperfield

Index

Ad Noise, 22–23, 29, 34
Agnew, Theo (Pinky), 61–62
Alexander, Fred, 28
Allen, Bill, 56, 97, 128, 144, 146, 149–51, 154–57
All-Men's Revue, 34
Alpha Phi, 70
American Conservatory of Music, 79
Andrews Sisters, the, 130
Anti-Saloon League, 13
Armstrong, Louis, 104
Avellana, Tony, 153

Baer, Lena, 46
Baker, Bonnie, 99
Ba-Na-Na, 150, 153
Battle Ground camp meetings, 16–17
Battle Ground Methodist Church, 11
Battle Ground, Indiana, 11, 16
Baugh, Ethridge B., 7
Beach Boys, 100
Beals, Kenny, 150
Benny, Jack, 100–101, 104, 105
Boone, Pat, 101
Branson, Gary, 151
"Brewers' Big Horses, The," 13
Britton, Milt, 99
Brown, Les, 99
Bryant, Bud, 42
Bugh, William, 85
Butler University, 130, 155

Caadd, Connie, 115
Cantor, Eddie, 106
Carnegie Hall, 1, 89, 111
Central Presbyterian Church (West Lafayette), 66, 70
Chapel Choir, 55
Cherry, Jeff, 150
Chicago Cubs, 41
Choral Club, 72, 73, 144, 149
Choraleers, 116
Christmas Shows, 75–77, 149
Cincinnati, University of, 150
Circle Theater (Indianapolis), 62
Clark, Wilma, 54
Clooney, Rosemary, 100
Cody, Buffalo Bill, 49
Cohee, Kenneth, 41
Cole, Nat King, 104
Colonna, Jerry, 103, 106
Columbus, Indiana, 156
Como, Perry, 130
Concert Choir, 58, 62
Cosby, Bill, 100
Covington, Indiana, 144
Crawfordsville, Indiana, 25–26, 28
Crosby, Bing, 100

Dadswell, Cyrus, 55
Dae, Donna, 7
Dartmouth College, 2, 7
Dean, Jimmy, 98
Debris, 55
Deckard, Wilma, 79
Delta Upsilon, 24, 36
DePauw University, 9, 24, 28–29, 33–39, 41, 45–46, 52, 70, 131–32
Ditamore, John, 101, 104
Dorsey, Tommy, 7, 100
Downs, Larry, 55
Duke University, 2
Durnell, Vassie, 94

Eastman Kodak Co., 112
Eddy, Nelson, 17
Eddy, Sonya Stewart, 79, 81, 101, 102, 116, 136

Electrical Engineering Building, 49, 60
Elizabeth II (queen of England), 123–24
Ellington, Duke, 100
Elliott, Edward C., 3, 49–50, 52–53, 56, 65–70, 79–80, 82–83, 86–87, 90, 92–93, 119
Elliott, Elizabeth, 67
Elliott Hall of Music, 1, 18, 75, 78, 80, 82, 84, 89, 92, 99, 145, 156
Elliott, Susan Bailey, 156
Elmhurst College, 2, 7
Erwin, Mark, 153
Ewbank, Darrell, 85

Farley, John, 97, 124
Feliciano, Jose, 100
First Methodist Church (West Lafayette), 18, 41
Fischang, William, 147
Fisher, Eddy, 106
Fisher, John, 129
Fitzgerald, Ella, 130
Flanagan, Art, 130
Ford, Bob, 141–42, 144, 148
Fort Wayne, Indiana, 147
Fosdick, Harry Emerson, 80
Fowler Hall, 20, 47, 50, 68–69, 75
Fox, Byron, 97
Frank, Edward, 56
Friend, Anna, 43
Friend, Bob, 43, 104
Friend, Josephine, 42
Friend, Lloyd, 43, 44
Friend, Mary, 42, 44
Friend, Paul (Dufe), 43
Friend, R. T., 43, 44, 45, 75
Friend, Ray, 43
Friend Sisters Trio, 42
Funk, Rosemary Robinson, 97

Gano, Kenny, 23
Gaylord, Jayne, 115
Gilbert and Sullivan, 42
Goldsmith, Arthur, 100
Goulet, Robert, 105
Greencastle, Indiana, 36, 45
Gunn, J. T., 56

"Hail Purdue," 55
Hall, Oakel, 29–30
Halleck, Charles, 121
Hansen, Arthur, 143
"Happy Wanderer, The," 123
Harlequin productions, 121
Hausenfluck, Larry, 71
Hawkins, Alma Williams, 47
Herman, Woody, 108
Hershey, Gen. Lewis, 90
High, Jack, 85
Hillis, Glen, 120–21
Hockema, Frank, 83, 121
Hole, Mary Lou, 94
Hollywood Bowl, 129
Hope, Bob, 100–101, 103, 106, 108
Hopf, Frank, 6
Hopper, Hedda, 106
Houston Symphony Chorale, 156
Hovde, Frederick, 75, 109
Hovde Hall of Administration, 49
Hummerickhouse, Mike, 150
Hunter, Chris, 136

Indiana Home Demonstration Chorus, 129
Indiana Society of Chicago, 120
Indiana Theater (Indianapolis), 62
Indiana University, 9, 50, 121, 142, 155
Israel, Jae, 151

Jacklin, Art, 6
Jazz Singer, The, 17
Jolson, Al, 17

Kaye, Danny, 100, 105
Kendall, Floyd, 22, 35
Kennedy, Bill, 6, 94
Kingma, Marilyn, 136
Kingston Trio, the, 100
Kirk, Chris, 150
Klimes, Dave, 150
Klinker, Kerri, 136
Klinker, Sheila Johnston, 130–31, 136
Knowles, Kenneth, 144
Kohls, Dick, 6
Krupa, Gene, 100
Kwasnieski, Alphonso, 94

La Guardia, Fiorello, 7
Lafayette Conservatory of Music, 46, 56
Lafayette Country Club, 101
Lafayette Life Insurance Co., 23–25, 28
Lake Freeman, 25
Lambert Fieldhouse, 6
Lambs' Club, 7
Lawrence, Steve, 130
Le Leur, John, 136
Lewis, Jerry, 108
Lewis, Jerry Lee, 130
Lilly, Joshua K., 57
Loeb, Bert, 100
Loepker, Tom, 150
Luhman, Bill, 47, 56, 97, 124, 128, 144, 146, 147–51, 152, 153, 156, 157
Luna Theater (Lafayette), 17–18, 42, 56

McCain, William, 85
McCutcheon High School, 155
McCutcheon, Robert, 26, 28, 36, 37, 38, 48, 52
McDonald, Beth, 136
MacDonald, Jeanette, 17
McGuire, Bruce (Mickey), 95, 96–97, 139, 142, 147, 149, 151

McKee Murray and Virginia, 66
McNair, Barbara, 98
McNeely, Joanna Stewart, 101, 102, 105, 116
Mantle, Mickey, 106
Mars Theater (Lafayette), 18, 22–23
Marshall Field's department stores, 128
Martin, Dean, 108
Martin, Dorothy (Doree), 94, 110, 116
Mathis, Johnny, 100
Men's Glee Club (Varsity Glee Club): at Carnegie Hall, 2–9; under Paul T. Smith, 18, 21; early organization of, 55; under Al Stewart, 56; as P.M.O. headliner, 68; impact of World War II on, 111–12; first international tour, 122–24; auditions, 124; summer camp, 128, 137; status in 1960s and 1970s, 141–42; changes under Luhman, 150
Mesta, Perle, 122
Methodist Hospital (Indianapolis), 14
Meyers, Marvin, 97, 129
Mill School (near Battle Ground), 11
Miller, Albert L., 11–12, 26, 27, 33–35, 66
Miller, Glenn, 111, 130
Mills, Edith, 70
Moeller, Edith, 123, 134
Monroe, Vaughn, 100
Montana, University of, 49
Monticello, Indiana, 25
Montmorenci, Indiana, 12
Moore, Richard, 29–30
Mortar Board Society, 47

Nalon, Chuck, 153
Nesius, Kitty, 115
Nixon, Richard, 143

Obernkirchen Children's Choir, 123
Oklahoma, University of, 2, 7
Onco, Frank, 2

Owen, Paul, 2
Owens, Sandra Parker, 156

Page, Patti, 101
Paramount Attractions (Chicago), 100
Pence, Indiana, 12
Perils of Pauline, 16
Peterson, Jim, 150
Physics Building, 49
Pielsticker, Erna, 123
"Pleasure Time," 1–2, 7
Poison Oaks, 150
Preston, Bobbie, 115
Prohibition, 13
Purdue Belles, 74, 149, 153
Purdue Memorial Union, 24–25, 60, 96
Purdue Mixed-Bell Choir, 149, 153
Purdue University Choir, 52, 56–57, 73, 144, 149
Purduettes, 110, 112–16, 130, 149, 156

Question Mark Convocation, 93

Ragains, Joseph, 70, 94
Ragains, Robert, 70
Raucous Trio, 150
Redlands, University of, 2
Remington, G. W., 55
Rochester, University of, 2, 7
Rogers, Ginger, 106
Ross-Ade Stadium, 49
Rotary Club, 112
Ryder, Henry, 94, 121

Schmidt–Hamann, Holger, 136, 138–39
Scholars, the, 136
Sheen, Fulton J., 80
Shelton, Doug, 150
Shoemaker, Carolyn, 47–48, 70
Shore, Dinah, 103
Sigma Phi Epsilon, 41–42

Silvers, Jack, 6
Simon and Garfunkel, 100
Simms, Ginny, 105
Sinatra, Frank, 100
Smith, Dick, 6, 97
Smith, George, 6
Smith, Helen Faust, 23, 41–42, 56
Smith, J. Peter (Pete Kelley), 94, 120–21
Smith, Jeanne St. Pierre, 129–30
Smith, Marvin, 2, 6, 7
Smith, Neil, 129–30
Smith, Paul T., 18, 21, 23, 55
Southworth's Bookstore, 52
Sportsman Hotel, 25
St. John's Church, 55
Stewart, Al: at Carnegie Hall, 2–9; birth of, 11; early music training of, 16; as Purdue student, 21–24; as head of Campus Commanders, 24–25; as DePauw student, 33–39; musical ability of, 35; courtship of Charlotte Friend, 42–43; teaching techniques, 46–47; first Purdue position, 47–48; first encounter with President Elliott, 50, 52–53; as director of Men's Glee Club, 56; Music Penthouse, 60–61; joins Purdue payroll, 65–66; marriage, 66; ability to size up audience, 68; Christmas Shows, 75–77; study in Chicago, 79–80; relationship with Elliott, 82–84, 86–87; as originator of Victory Varieties, 99; celebrity contacts, 105; extension music, 128–29; industrial music, 128–29; at Republican convention, 129; honorary degree, 131–32; secrets of singing, 132; retirement, 144–45. *See also* photos on pages 10, 15, 32, 88, 91, 94, 98, 102, 103, 104, 140, 143
Stewart, Austin (brother), 14, 15
Stewart, Charlotte Friend (wife), 6, 40, 41–44, 65–67, 79, 81, 91, 102, 138, 143

Stewart, Delmar (brother), 14, 15
Stewart, Ethel Pearson (mother), 11, 14, 15, 16–17, 28, 36, 76, 102
Stewart, Glenn (brother), 14, 15, 16, 22, 25, 28–29, 42
Stewart, Joanna (daughter). *See* McNeely, Joanna Stewart
Stewart, Lillian, 57, 60
Stewart, Lillian Balkema (wife of Glenn), 29
Stewart, Olin Scott (father), 11–14, 15
Stewart, R. B., 57, 60, 80, 99
Stewart, Sonya (daughter). *See* Eddy, Sonya Stewart
Stone, Winthrop, 49
Stravinsky, Igor, 108
Strite, Jack, 136
Sullivan, Ed, 100
Swartz, Wendell, 85, 122

Tam, Robert, 85
Terre Haute, Indiana, 25, 28
Thompson, Diane, 146, 151, 155
Trinity Methodist Church (Crawfordsville), 26, 27
Tyler, Horace, 85

University Hall, 57, 60, 69

Vagabonds, the, 99
Vallee, Rudy, 92
Valparaiso University, 11
Vaught, Sally Grigsby, 156
Victory Varieties, 99–109

Wabash College, 26
Waldorf Astoria, 7
Waring, Fred, 1, 2, 5, 7, 8, 89, 100–101, 133
Warnicke, Rene, 129
Washington and Lee University, 2, 7
Washington, Indiana, 150
Waveland, Indiana, 12, 14
Wesley Foundation (West Lafayette), 41
West Lafayette High School, 17–18, 24
Whitcomb, Pamela Wendt, 156
Whitcomb, Steve, 156
Whiteman, Paul, 25
Williams, Paul, 98
Wilson, Bob, 7
Wilson, Jean, 7
Winstead, Roger, 153
WLFI (West Lafayette television station), 142
WLS (Chicago radio station), 45
Wolin, Sandy, 94
Women's Glee Club, 47–49, 51, 54, 55
Wotawa, E. J., 55
Wynn, Ed, 18

Yoke, Cal, 136
Young, Jack, 97
Yount, Dennis, 73, 149, 151, 155

Zissis, Cecelia, 130

To:
Lois Gotwals,
With sincere appreciation
and thanks —
Bill Adler